Mary Lou's Mindset

A JOURNEY OF DETERMINATION, COURAGE AND FAITH

Michelle L. Washington

WORKBOOK PRESS LLC
187 E Warm Springs Rd,
Suite B285 Las Vegas NV 89119 USA

Website: https://workbookpress.com/
Hotline: 1-888-818-4856
Email: admin@workbookpress.com

Ordering Information:

Quantity sales. Special discounts are available on quantity purchases by corporations, associations, and others. For details, contact the publisher at the address above.

Library of Congress Control Number:

ISBN-13:   978-1-965732-16-8   Paperback Version
              978-1-965732-17-5   Hardback Version
              978-1-965732-18-2   Digital Version

REV. DATE: 08/22/2024

Mary Lou's Mindset

A JOURNEY OF DETERMINATION, COURAGE AND FAITH

Michelle L. Washington

INTRODUCTION

One of the greatest women that ever graced the face of this earth was born on July 2, 1925 in Clay, Kentucky. She was great not because of any fortune or fame as most consider wealth. Her greatness was due to her mental perseverance, "personal pluckiness" and boldness to believe in an unseen God, despite unbelievable odds. She was quick to tell anyone about the rationale behind her birthright to blessings. In this one sentence of simplicity she would define the aura of her resilience by saying,

"I'm the seventh child and I was born in the seventh month."

To her, it made perfect sense, because the number seven is biblically known to be the special number of God that symbolizes perfection. In the Bible, the number seven has been significantly used to do and represent many special and miraculous things.

In the life of Mary Louise (Mary Lou) Battle, it was evidenced that her position of being born as the seventh child and also being born in July, the seventh month, brought her an extra special surrounding of blessings, even in the darkest of days. For this reason alone, I personally gave her the nickname, ***"Lucky Seven".***

Whenever I witnessed Mother come through a hardship of great difficulty, amidst insurmountable obstacles, I would immediately say,

"Look at you, Lucky Seven".

Even in the most ordinary days of doing the most ordinary tasks, like going to the grocery store, pumping gas or visiting the thrift stores, I saw easy blessings fall into the hands of my Mother, Mary Lou.

She often would step out of her car and find money right at her feet while opening her car door. Then she would enter the store and walk right to marked down items which were sometimes even being discounted as she approached the store merchandise. Most surprisingly was the day that I accompanied her to Kmart to pick up a few items. Shortly after entering the store, she told another shopper, who was a total stranger, that she liked her purse. Immediately, the lady said, *"You can have it."*

My Mom told her, *"No, that's okay. You keep your purse."* However, the lady was insistent that my Mother receive the purse and made her keep it. Right at that instant, the lady emptied all of the items from her purse with a great big smile and gave it directly to my Mother.

Now that was truly out of the ordinary. I had never witnessed anything like that with anyone. It also shocked my Mom. Somehow these type of blessings were never really a coincidence or just happenstance, because each morning Mary Lou prayed,

"Make me a blessing to someone today, Lord."
This daily prayer of Mary Lou came from the following song which says,

Make Me a Blessing
Verse 1

Out in the high-ways and by-ways of life,
Many are weary and sad;
Carry the sunshine where darkness is rife,
Making the sorrowing glad.

CHORUS:

Make me a blessing, Make me a blessing.
Out of my life May Jesus shine.
Make me a blessing, O Savior, I pray,
Make me a blessing to someone today.

Verse 2

Tell the sweet story of Christ and His love.
Tell of His power to forgive.
Others will trust Him if only you prove
True, every moment you live.

Verse 3

Give as 'twas given to you in your need,
Love as the Master loved you.
Be to the helpless a helper indeed.
Unto your mission be true.

Author of Lyrics:
Ira B. Wilson, 1909
The you tube link below has the recorded song.
https://youtu.be/j2cRbOqrhb4?si=6C-K9oJnUrhcjme7

Lou Hemingway, Lawrence Jacobs and Sadie Jacobs survey bags of food for the needy.

Mary Lou was all about giving of herself to be a blessing to everyone that she could. In the collage above, she is volunteering with Lawrence and Sadie Jacobs to give free food donations and commodities at Oakwood University Church Food Storehouse.

Mary Lou sang with the Church Chorale, worked with the Oakwood University Church Hospitality Committee and served as a Pathfinder Master Guide while a Pastor's Wife in the Birmingham, Alabama suburban areas. **Pictorial Credits for Oakwood University Church Storehouse and Church Chorale Photos: The Huntsville Times**

Amazingly, the irony of her genuinely wanting to be a blessing, often gave her more blessings than she ever expected. So often, did she receive blessings.

She received so many until Mom was always giving something away to others. Her mindset of giving, allowed her to daily manifest the essence of one of her favorite texts found in *Acts 20: 35* which says,

"for it is more blessed to give than to receive."

So what's so different about the story of this "depression era" born woman who survived great odds like many of her family, friends and associates of that hardship time? In a simple explanation, it was the beauty, consistency, and unselfishness of her tenacity despite the oppression, suppression and at times depression within her life. It was purely the resilient *"Mindset of Mary Lou"* that made her spirit joyous and her life monumentally firm. Beyond all of that, it was her heartfelt faith in God that gave her the miraculous mindset that she daily chose to live with. Our Mother's determination was anchored in the Lord whom she loved and also in whom she believed in, regardless of her difficult journeys.

Lastly, these reflections share my desires for my Mother's story throughout many years.

The growing up promise that I made to my Mother, when I was a girl, was that one day, I was going to write her story and share it with others. She would often look at me and chuckle. Then as she leisurely shrugged her shoulders, she would say, "Michelle my story is no different from any one else's. I just did what I had to do."

To me, that is what made my Mother's story so extra special. The fact that she was not defeated by the problems that had surrounded her life, made her even more amazing to me. It was not because she was my Mother that I gravitated to her story, but because she was a woman with a tremendous amount of persevering strength, resilience and faith in God.

As the decades passed and I had the opportunity to see my Mother sojourn through great difficulties, I found her mindset to be an inspirational gift, not only to me but also to those whom she shared her encouragement with. With that said, I invite you to sojourn through my Mother's journey of struggle, sorrow, love, joy, discouragement, confrontation, strength and peace.

May her journey, "Mary Lou's Mindset", be one that leaves you with the reminder of truth in the old saying, "Mind over Matter". That is also what determines the quality of our experiences, because, what we choose to believe, truly does make a monumental difference in the journey of what we call life.

DEDICATION PAGE

This book is dedicated to the unforgettable woman and also the remarkable memories that it represents of Mary Louise Battle. This dedication could only find itself honoring the life that has been so clearly portrayed within each chapter. It is my hope that each reader will find the reality of my Mother's mindset throughout each and every challenge that my Mother experienced. Ultimately, I desire that those who read this life script will unite with the same tenacious determination that held Mary Lou close to the convictions of her heart.

This collage is in Memory of my Mother, Mary Louise Battle (Washington) Hemingway

ABOUT THE AUTHOR

Michelle L. Washington started her professional journey over 40 years ago, as an elementary teacher, after graduating from Oakwood College in 1982. Since that time she has been blessed to share her talents and skills with children in Pre-K through 8th grade classrooms all over the country. During this journey, Michelle has had a passion for building literacy skills and she also has invested in supporting an initial language arts foundation among early learners.

Michelle's first book was entitled:

A Treasury of African American ABC's and Nursery Rhymes for Children.

By Michelle L. Washington
Graphics by Corel Corporation

That book (now out of print) has a copy of an official letter from former President Bill Clinton.

This biography about **Mary Lou's Mindset**, is a journey that has been shared to remind readers everywhere about the importance of hope, resilience and diligence regardless of one's life experiences. Michelle's promise to her Mother about writing Mary Lou's life journey has now been fulfilled. As you read, may you connect to the various sojourns within this historical journey of almost 9 decades. Thank you for selecting this biography for your personal library.

FOREWORD

It is not often that one gets the opportunity and privilege to write the Foreword on behalf of their Mother's Biography. With that said, it gives me great pleasure to share this with you.

My Mother, Mary Lou Battle (Washington) Hemingway was a loving and loyal wife, mother, family member, church member, friend and also a very unique individual. She shared so many wonderful adventures with those whom she loved. Because of her generous spirit and loving personality, Mary Lou left those whom she fondly surrounded, with unforgettable and cherished lifetime memories.

She explained to me when I was in the third grade why I had two maternal grandmothers. Through the years I learned more about them and the blessings that they provided. As her first born child and only son, I was also able to experience a part of her lifetime journey that was a result of her *one of a kind story.*

Michelle, my youngest sister has been blessed with a special, God given, literary gift. It is because of Michelle's talent, as well as her amazing dedication and love for our mother, that she has written this timelessly inspiring journey and intriguing biography, entitled, *Mary Lou's Mindset.*

This literary journey takes you from the humble hollows of Clay, Kentucky, to the big city life in Cleveland, Ohio. Then later on you will learn of Mary Lou's sojourn to Oakwood College, located in Huntsville, Alabama, where her life would be greatly and *forever impacted.*

Michelle has expertly captured these precious experiences in photos and in writing. As you read *Mary Lou's Mindset,* you will vividly see and feel her determination, courage and faith.

It was beyond pleasure to have her as our Mother and I am grateful for the spiritual beliefs that she taught me regarding Jesus' Second Coming. I have that blessed hope and assurance that soon and very soon we will be reunited in Heaven. What a day of rejoicing that will be.

Hubert D. Washington,
Retired Educator & Administrator

This photo was taken in 1998 with my Mother, my brother, Hubert and I in Huntsville, Alabama during Easter Weekend. It was also Oakwood University's Alumni Weekend. Photography Credits: Olan Mills Studio

STATEMENT OF AUTHENTICATION

The authenticity of our Mother's Biography, *Mary Lou's Mindset*, has been accurately written and is a totally true, nonfiction and historical account of events that happened in her life.

As Mary Lou's eldest and first born child I, Hubert Dale Washington, do declare with sound mind and without any issues of memory loss, that all of the stories were still amazingly vivid in our Mother's mind even right before her death.

Hubert D. Washington
April 11, 2021

TABLE OF CONTENTS

King James Bible

"Before I formed thee in the belly I knew thee; and before thou carriest forth out of the womb, I sanctified thee." Jeremiah 1:5

New International Version

For you created my inmost being; you knit me together in my mother's womb.

Psalms 139:13

CHAPTER 1
Blessings Before Birth

"Prenatal Abandonment"

One may wonder, *"What kind of a woman vows to give her very own baby away to her childless sister-in-law before she has even gotten pregnant?"*

To add to this story,

"What woman makes that kind of a promise without communicating that kind of vow to her husband, who is also going to be the biological father of the prospective child to be given away?"

That may sound odd, however that was the confidential arrangement that was in place between my Grandmother, Pearl Battle and her sister-in-law, Mary Louise (Washington) Battle, sometime around the year of 1924.

At some point before October of 1924, my Grandmother Pearl decided that she was tired of raising children. She was dealing with child *number six*. According to the handed down account of her life and also documentation, she had become a wife at 18, on December 16, 1909. Then she quickly became a Mother a year later at 19, for the first time, in 1910. Between 1910 and 1922, after already having six children, four girls and two boys, Pearl was tired of the frequency of her pregnancies. One can only imagine the physical, emotional and psychological fatigue she experienced from trying to fulfill her role as a teenage wife and Mother.

Pearl and Joel Clarence Battle are seen in this photo sometime during 1913, with their first three children, who were all daughters. Left to right is Daisy, the eldest of their nine children, then there's Baby Cassie, sitting in Pearl's lap. Standing in front of Joel is the second eldest, Hazel, who looked exactly like Joel and who she always called "Papa".

Pearl's six child births prior to 1925, spanned these time frames: *Daisy Lloyd-***1910**, *Hazel Ernestine-***1912**, *Cassie Beatrice-* **1913**, *Mattie Jane-***1917**, *Calvin Clarence -***1919**, *and Felix Alfred-***1922**. **Having been born December 14, 1891, Pearl was around 31 in 1922.**

Consider the brutalities of Pearl's youthful era as she was being not only a woman, but at the same time, "a negro woman". With the well known historical knowledge of our American abuses, injustices, inequalities, bigotry, brutalities and chauvinism, Pearl had much to deal with. She had a lot to deal with, not only because of her gender, but also because of her race. No one knows what her exact sentiments were when she told her childless, sister-in- law, Mary Louise these words,

"If the next baby I have is a girl, I'm going to give her to you and name her after you."

The one thing that is known, is that the two women kept their secret and they did not share it with anyone, not even with their own husbands, who were biologically blood brothers. Little did either of the women realize how their commitment to this secret would impact not only both of their lives but also an entire family. They were only focused on the desires of their hearts. Yet, the power of fulfilling their hearts desires would eventually break some of their deepest heartstrings in the future days to come.

Mary Louise Washington Battle, who my siblings and I affectionately called, "Grandmother Mary Lou", was married to Pearl's husband's older brother, Wright Battle. Pearl was married to Joel Battle, Wright's younger brother. Grandmother Pearl and Grandpa Joel, had no problem with procreation. Remember, they already had *six,* healthy children around 1924.

On the other hand, Grandmother Mary Lou and her husband Wright, who we called "Uncle Wright" had no children to call their own. To make matters even worse, it was said among the elders of the Battle Family that Uncle Wright did have many children. However, not any of them were born from Grandmother Mary Lou.

This kind of emptiness from not bearing children was not an experience that Mary Louise felt good about. Being a loving woman, with so much kindness, left her heart with so much goodness to share. Surrounded by the bountiful births of Pearl could only make Mary Louise yearn even more so for a child of her own that she could love, nurture, mentor, and raise.

From this viewpoint one may wonder if Pearl was feeling somewhat sorry for her sister-in- law's childless state. Pearl was well aware of how Wright had fathered several children with women other than his wife, Mary Louise. As a fertile, child bearing woman, could Pearl have felt some kind of empathy toward Mary Louise, her barren sister- in- law who could not bear even one child for Wright Battle?

Pictured above is Wright Battle on the far left, who was the husband of Mary Louise, brother of Joel Battle and uncle of Mary Lou. Pictured standing with him, to the right, are his siblings, Mary Etta, Joel Clarence and Albert. At the very end is Calvin Battle, Mary Lou's eldest brother. They are standing on their own Battle heir property which is located in Newellton, Louisiana.

Had there been a Facebook back in their day, the status of Mary Louise and Wright's marriage may have surpassed "it's complicated" to "it's scandalous". From all that I have ever been told, I truly believe that the two women had formed a bond of loyalty out of a necessity to find empathy which was scarce within both of their lives. They needed a place of comfortable understanding that "the great depression era" would not bring to the innermost chambers of their minds. And so, the deal was made and it came into play when Pearl's "7th child", Mary Louise Battle, better known as "Mary Lou", was born.

Mary Lou Washington-Battle
"Little Mama"

   This is a lovely photo of Mary Louise Washington Battle, better known as "Little Mama" or "Grandmother Mary Lou". In this picture, Mary Louise is a student at Oakwood Training School. (Now known as Oakwood University, a "HBCU", Historic Black College University) While a student, she met Ellen G. White, Prophetess and Author from the Seventh-day Adventist Church. *See pages 279 & 280 for more about Ellen White's life.

   Grandmother Mary Lou was a domestic worker. Once hired, she was favored because her meals were not only very visually appealing, but also very deliciously pleasing. Mixed with her kind, respectful, quiet and honest spirit, few could be unsatisfied with the level of service that Grandmother Mary Lou provided. To have worked within the homes of some of Cleveland's, "Lake Drive Affluence", during such an era of economic depravity, speaks volumes about the quality of work that she demonstrated.

Secondly, Grandmother Mary Lou was allowed to bring food home with her from her job and that is exactly what she did. She brought consistent amounts of good food home and took it to feed Pearl during her seventh pregnancy. Mary Louise fed Pearl so well that by the time "Baby Mary Lou" was born, she came into this world weighing over 12 pounds.

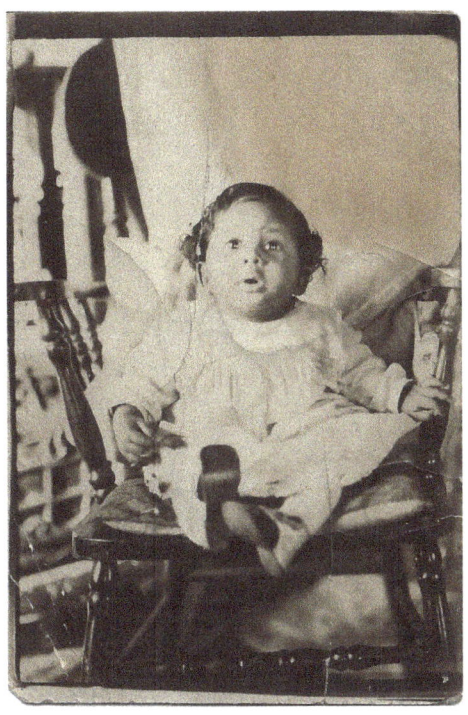

This is a picture of Baby Mary Lou around three months old. She looked like her father Joel and his family.

One of the very first blessings that Mary Louise had given to Baby Mary Lou was bestowed before she came out of her birth mother's (Pearl's) womb. Mary Lou had the prenatal nutrition from the pantries of wealthy white women at a time when food was sparse to most Americans suffering within a depressed economy. (At the time of Pearl's pregnancy, Pearl, Mary Louise and their husbands were living in Kentucky because Mary Lou was born in Clay, Kentucky.)

As the biblical "Baby Moses" was fed by the blessings of an Egyptian Princess, "Baby Mary Lou" was also fed from a wealthy table where food was plentiful. Her awaiting assigned Mother, Mary Louise, was committed to giving Mary Lou the very best that she could at the first knowledge of Pearl's pregnancy. This committed mindset of faithfulness was forever at the essence of whatever Grandmother Mary Lou sacrificed to give to her promised daughter of arrangement, even during the prenatal stages of Baby Mary Lou's care.

This position of faith was also at the foundation of the belief system that Mary Louise chose to exercise. Without the knowledge of what gender the baby would be, Mary Louise acted as though Pearl was going to have a baby girl. Earnestly wanting to have a child so badly, gave Mary Louise hope beyond any thought that Pearl's 7th baby could have been a boy. This childless woman had set her heart upon receiving Pearl's baby. Only Heaven knows what the anticipation was like for Mary Louise as she waited for those nine months to pass by.

It was 1925 and there were no sonograms for Pearl to receive as indications of her seventh child's gender. Without hope, faith and constant prayer, Mary Louise could not have survived this waiting period of not knowing if she would actually be able to benefit from Pearl's pregnancy. Remember, the conditions of Pearl's "baby arrangement" was wrapped in the fact that the baby given to Mary Louise must be a girl. So imagine the greatness of "expectant faith" which Mary Louise must have had to consistently bring food to Pearl for nine months. This is a deep indicator as to the heartfelt prayers of Mary Louise. With great faith, she believed that Pearl's womb would produce the baby girl that she was hoping to receive.

Despite Pearl's choice to silently scheme and plot against Joel, her own husband, Pearl's heart was definitely one of unbelievable courage and to some, Pearl's heart exemplified a very, small degree of wisdom. I say this because Pearl's arrangement, which was calculated upon the condition of only giving Mary Louise a baby girl, was probably based upon the fact that she knew Joel would not have ever watched one of his baby boys being given away to anyone. Nevertheless, to even assume that Joel would have any attitude of acceptance toward parting with any of his children, regardless of gender, was truly an unwise assumption for Pearl to ever ponder.

As it was, Joel never accepted the fact that Pearl had even considered and then connived to make the decision that she had made about his seventh child and baby girl, in the first place. Once he eventually found out, Joel's heart was forever broken from Pearl's secretive choice to give his baby girl away to their sister- in-law, Mary Louise.

The heart of Joel was so broken that he would, 21 years later, in June of 1947, refuse to give Mary Lou away on her wedding day. Mary Lou's wedding was not attended by Joel. He did not share one of the most important days of his daughter's life with her because he had not ever been able to fully share his rightful patriarchal position as Mary Lou's Father.

Yet, Joel Battle did give this daughter of his heart and heritage, a crisp, *one-hundred-dollar bill* on the day of her wedding, according to Mary Lou. Back in those days, that was truly like a great financial treasury towards beginning a new marriage. In today's present "2024 economy", the worth of that 1947, $100.00 bill would have had the purchasing power equal to $1347.06.

Considering those financial factors, Joel Battle was letting Mary Lou know that he wanted her to not only have his well wishes, but also his well-intended financial send off as she started her marital life.

Although still brokenhearted, after almost 22 years of watching Mary Lou grow up outside of his home, Joel still wanted Mary Lou to know that he loved her and wished her "his best" on her wedding day. As Mary Lou shared her own wedding memories, she said,

"Papa wouldn't give me away, but I will never forget how he surprised me when he showed up to specifically give me that crisp one-hundred-dollar bill on my wedding day. After he pulled it out and placed it in my hand, he then quietly left."

That day of such monumental significance was not normal for Mary Lou or Joel. It held a silent shadow that would not remove itself from family history. As happy as a wedding day should be, can you imagine yourself being the bride and not having your father walk you down the aisle to your groom and soon to be husband? For Mary Lou, this was another moment of keeping her mind focused upon the bigger picture. She could have chosen a different outlook and let that disappointment take effect. But, her love for Joel and the respect that she had always carried in her heart for him, gave her an empathy and outlook of understanding for how he had felt about the entire situation. With that focus, Mary Lou projected onward.

Joel's seventh child was being given away for the second time. This time it was for a lifetime commitment of marriage where parents are no longer responsible. What could Joel have been thinking on that wedding day, when he had never been included or considered in "the first give away" when Mary Lou was a baby?

Mary Lou and Hugh's wedding, June 1947 Photographer Credits: Mr. Lucian Dixon Left to right: Irene Miller Walker, Marcelle Martin Edmond, (Mary Lou and Hugh) Felix Battle, James Palmer, and Marilyn Harris (Flower Girl)

There are times when words are far beyond the emotions within one's heart. Those unspoken words stand in the silence of time and space without the desire for explanations. Yet, that silence cannot excuse what appears to be the absence of love, when love still truly exists deeply beyond any words. For Joel Battle and Mary Lou, his precious daughter that had been gifted away, without his paternal consent or knowledge, that wedding day held one of those undeniable moments of *unspeakable love.*

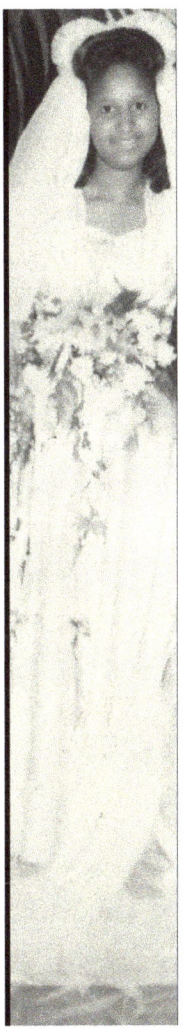

Imagine being in Joel Battle's patriarchal position on Mary Lou's Wedding Day. Seeing your biological daughter as a beautiful bride, yet walking away on one of her happiest days, that must have been one of the hardest days of Joel's fatherhood.

The initial trauma of one of Joel's greatest disappointments in life centered in the Spring of 1926. Before Mary Lou turned one-year-old, Pearl surrendered her beautiful baby girl to Mary Louise. It was as though a tsunami wave had hit Joel Battle's household when he found out what his wife Pearl had promised to his brother's wife, Mary Louise. That one promissory act of surrender brought a breach between my grandparents that would never be repaired. As if the emotional impact of the secrecy alone was not injurious enough to the pride of Joel Battle's manhood and paternalistic instincts, the fact that his very own little baby girl came into the world looking just like him, his favorite sister, and his family, added insult to the already grievous injury of losing one of his children.

Joel responded to Pearl's arrangement by departing from his home. He did not depart from his role as the father of his children and often made visits to see his family. In later years, Joel made his permanent home in Newellton, Louisiana where his family owned many acres of heir property. His love for Pearl never seemed to totally wane. Although he chose separation from Pearl, neither Joel or Pearl ever sought a legal separation or divorce. In fact, Joel and Pearl had an eighth child after Mary Lou. Pearl's last pregnancy with Joel was a boy who was named after Joel's father, Henry. Her last pregnancy was a girl, whom Pearl named Catherine after her mother.

Beautiful Aunt Mary Etta was Joel Battle's favorite sister and one of Mary Lou's favorite aunts. Handsome Uncle Dave (David Battle) was one of Grandpa Joel's brothers who treated Mary Lou like she was his very own daughter.

Joel Battle's siblings are pictured above attending a family reunion in New London, Ohio. Pictured right to left are: Albert, David, Mary Etta, Laura, and Georgia. Georgia's husband, Morris Battle is on the left end. (Uncle Morris was from a different Battle Family who was not related to Joel's family. However, it was ironic that he had the same last name of "Battle." Uncle Morris' parents, Felix and Catherine Battle had 18 children. Pearl, Mary Lou's "birth mother" was one of those 18 children and for that reason, Pearl and Morris were sister and brother.)

This is Henry Battle, the Battle Patriarch and Father of Joel C. Battle. Henry was also Mary Lou's Paternal Grandfather. He was the father of over 12 children. *Five* of Great Grandfather Henry's adult children are seen in the previous picture.

This collage represents *five generations of the Battle Lineage* beginning with Great Grandfather Henry, on to Grandpa Joel Clarence, then on to Mary Louise and then finally Hubert Dale and his son Jonathan Scott.

Joel **"NEVER"** got over the choice that Pearl made without his knowledge and consent. It was something that he not only lived with throughout his entire lifetime, but also held within his heart, as an unspoken wound. Joel loved his daughter, Mary Lou dearly, but every time he looked at her whenever she came to visit, he was reminded of the deceit that had not even given him an option to have a choice or a voice in a decision that was rightfully his to refute.

Even now as I look back into my childhood and remember our Grandfather Joel visiting our home, I cannot ever forget the way he silently looked at our Mother with an inner depth that only time could have accounted for. His silent stare was one that left an emptiness of wonderment where words had no welcome, because there was all of that brokenness within his heart. What had been taken from his fatherhood could not ever be replaced within any visit that he made to our home. Those years of cradling, nurturing and loving his baby girl, while daily watching her develop under his paternal watch care were stripped from him by the heartless choices of his very own wife and sister-in-law.

My Aunt Hazel always said,

*"If Papa (Joel) had known what Mama (Pearl) was going to do, he would have **NEVER** stood for it. He didn't know that Mama was going to give Mary Lou away to Aunt Mary Lou. When he found out, he was madder than a wet hen and Papa was so hurt, that things were never ever the same between Mama and Papa. That one decision from Mama was the main thing that separated our parents for life."*

This is a picture of our wonderful and loving Grandfather, Joel Clarence Battle in May 1973 attending our sister, Marla Lynne's Graduation. Mary Lou was so thrilled to have "her Papa" present for the occasion. Joel came all the way from Newellton, Louisiana to attend Marla's High School Graduation. (Adelphian Academy in Holly, Michigan)

But being promised to Grandmother Mary Louise was truly a blessing to Mary Lou. As she was fed with blessings of the very best food from Mary Louise, while in Pearl's womb, Mary Lou would also be fed spiritual, cultural, emotional and social graces that could only come from a woman of great Christian maturity, morality and mannerisms. That woman was not the Mother of her birth, but rather, the Mother of her blessings, Mary Louise Washington Battle. As the years continued, Mary Louise would prove herself to be one of the greatest blessings not only before the birth of her promised and pre- arranged daughter, but also throughout Mary Lou's lifetime.

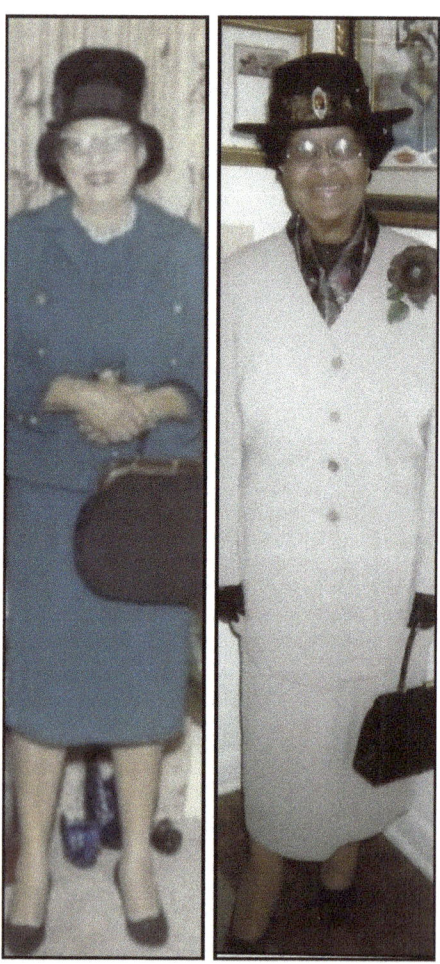

This is a 1950's picture of Joel Battle's favorite sister, Aunt Mary Etta, on the left.

Mary Lou is on the right. It reveals how Mary Lou truly favored her Father's family even in her senior years. The picture was taken in Mary Lou's Huntsville Home in 2005.

King James Bible

Remember now thy Creator in the days of thy youth, while the evil days come not, nor the years draw nigh, when thou shalt say, I have no pleasure in them; Ecclesiastes 12:1

New International Version

Can a mother forget the baby at her breast and have no compassion on the child she has borne? Though she may forget, I will not forget you! See I have engraved you on the palms of my hands; your walls are ever before me.

Isaiah 49:15 & 16

CHAPTER 2
Blooming Beyond Blessings

"From Depression Era Child to Jim Crow Adolescent"

Some of the earliest accounts from my Mother's depression era childhood were the visits that she made to see her siblings and her parents, Joel and Pearl Battle. If truth was stranger than fiction, then it definitely was so in the mind of young Mary Lou. Trying to wrap her mind around the fact that she was the only one of 9 children that was given away, was a great challenge to Mary Lou's Mindset. That was challenging not just only in her childhood, but also throughout stages of her adulthood.

How does one wrestle through that fact of being promised to be given away (before conception) and still find true validity on the other side of stable reasoning? Even more, how can one ever truly feel safe, affirmed and accepted among their birth family, when they are at the center of controversial decisions that have been rooted in deep arenas of deceitful transactions which occurred without their involvement?

Although Mary Lou was a vibrant, blessed and beautiful child, she could not exchange any of her underlying and unanswered questions for all of the vibrancy, beauty and talent in the entire world. The depression era times were hard enough, but then add the unexpected emotional experiences that troubled Mary Lou's mind on certain occasions when she went back home. One of those moments that left a tremendous impact was when Mary Lou became a witness to one of her parents' arguments. She remembered, even at 88 years of age, the vividness of that argument and she told the story just as if it had just happened exactly one day before she had recounted it. The depth of the argument between her parents became so heated that Mary Lou said,

"Papa got so angry with Mama that he took the hatchet and chased Mama while she ran away screaming. I don't know exactly what he was mad about. All I remember is that it had something to do with a report that Papa got from my school. What I do know is that I had never seen him that angry before."

Being seven years old made the intensity of that argument even more horrific for a little girl who knew that she was somehow a huge part of the reason for her parents' separation. Not only were there internal and external conflicts between Joel and Pearl, but there were also the moments of struggle behind the issues of visiting between two families.

Even the awkward feelings of remorse that Mary Lou's siblings had every time she had to leave and go back home where she lived with Mary Louise (who she at times referred to as "Little Mama"), was also a part of the difficulties surrounding her developmental years. Aunts Hazel and Cassie, two of Mary Lou's sisters explained the situation like this,

"We all loved our sister, Mary Lou and we never understood why Mother gave her to Aunt Mary Lou. It bothered us, but we didn't really talk about it. We just tried

to show Mary Lou how much we loved her and we did everything that we could to make her feel that she was our sister in spite of what Mother had done."

As I watched my own Mother listen to her sisters explain this to me, it pierced my soul to see how deeply it still touched my Mother. Even at the age of being a senior citizen at the time of that conversation, and into her seventies, the questioning expression on her face, as well as the silent shrug of her shoulders, marked with a slant of her head toward the right, spoke volumes to me about "the lifetime silence" that had occurred in regards to Grandmother Pearl's decision.

An entire family had lived with a matriarchal force that was greater than their ability to express themselves. And even after her death, it appeared in that instance that Pearl Battle's decision held enough power to still silence the feelings of those she had disappointed and hurt. Her absence, even in her death, had still remained a force of power over her daughter's lives. That speaks volumes about the powerful effects of a Mother's decisions.

So how did Mary Lou bloom beyond even the blessings of an "assigned Mother" who wanted the very best for her? This is where the significance of her birth order, number and also the number of her birth month, "number seven" holds miraculous weight. In some of the worst of times, Mary Lou had opportunities that she only could have had, because of providential moments of blessing from the God that she believed in and prayed to. Mary Lou went to *eight* different schools within twelve years of attending Grade 1 through her senior year at Central High in Cleveland. The continual transitory state that she experienced was mainly due to the changes made by Mary Louise within several domestic work assignments.

Then right before becoming a teenager, Mary Lou witnessed one of the most devastating examples of betrayal from her "assigned father" and uncle, Wright Battle. One day, within the quietness of the early morning sleeping hours, Wright slipped out the house taking the car, the sewing machine, typewriter and every item of significant value with him, in order to abruptly flee his marriage with Mary Louise. In one simple sentence my Mother said,

"That hurt Mama so bad and she never said too much about it to me."

Everything that Mary Louise had struggled hard to secure for her family was stolen by the same thief who had stolen her heart and also whom she had married, loved, trusted and treasured.

Now once again, where blessings had been in place, blooming had to transpire. Blooms don't ever exist without some kind of struggle. There are stages of blooming and there are evolutions of "persistent pushing" before blooming takes place.

There were many things that Mary Lou had to push through during this transitory growth period of her life. Although she may have had many uncertainties about Pearl's decision, God used her assigned Mother, Mary Louise to validate His Plan for her life.

Mary Lou's "Little Mama", {Mary Louise} **never grew tired** *of validating her assigned daughter that Pearl had given her. The Godly Love that Mary Louise consistently poured out upon Mary Lou was a monumental force that helped fortify her teenage mindset amidst inner conflict. Where Mary Lou may have had normal doubts about herself, Mary Louise gave her the positive reassurance to remember that God had not forgotten her.*

And so in this growth phase and pre-adolescent stage of her life, Mary Lou was determined to work as hard as she could to help Mary Louise. She wanted to be a blessing to the Mother who had faithfully sacrificed so much for her and always without any complaint. So Mary Lou worked right beside Mary Louise fulfilling domestic demands while serving in some of the finest mansions of Cleveland, Ohio.

It was somewhere around this time that the African American singer, dancer and actress, Ethel Waters met Mary Lou while visiting one of the mansions where Mary Louise was working. Ethel Waters was more to that era than what Beyoncé is to this era. She was among the highest paid African Americans of that time and that was beyond huge when one considers the financial impact upon all Americans in the Great Depression.

As seen in the next pictures, Ethel Waters was an unbelievable woman with unprecedented status. She was not only a trailblazer, but even more so, a groundbreaking chisel. Her relevance was tremendously impactful beyond racial, financial and gender expectations of that American timeframe. At a time when Americans were standing in bread lines to receive food rations, what Ethel Waters was able to achieve was amazingly beyond incredible.

America's Motion Picture Industry has yet to leave a historical account of the tremendous legacy and stellar sacrifices given by this one citizen of courage. This is a true oversight that needs to be changed so that this legendary lady's lifetime contributions and brilliance will be visually shared with future generations on the large screen.

Both of these photos are taken during the early career of Ethel Waters when she was extremely successful and famous during the years of America's "Great Depression".

Photo Credits: Google Images

This is an actual autographed photo of Ethel Waters which I purchased and own. *It is taken from the 1933 musical comedy revue,* ***"As Thousands Cheer".***

Of even more significance of her status, is the fact that Ethel Waters had to break barriers of racial discrimination, bigotry, and scorn while becoming one of the highest paid Negro performers of her time.

For a woman of Ethel Waters national notoriety and stature to make such a request to Mary Louise for Mary Lou's temporary guardianship, was a *huge* as well as a generous proposition. Moreover, it was especially so in those days when things were so very lean across the entire nation.

According to my older brother, Hubert, our Mother shared her memories about this experience just a few months before she passed away in 2013. He said that they were reminiscing about his boyhood and how the family would take trips from Toledo to Cleveland.

Hubert shared that while he was recounting one of the trips that he and our parents made back to Cleveland, he reminded my Mother of the time that she had our Father take them along Lake Avenue so that she could show Hubert where she had gone to elementary school for one year. She also pointed out some of the actual mansions where she had lived with Grandmother Mary Lou who had been a live-in domestic cook.

This is the actual account of how Hubert described his memories of that conversation with our Mother.

"As I reflect on my Mother, Mary Lou and how special she was, I am reminded of a conversation we had during her last remaining months of life. She very vividly reminisced about her childhood growing up in Cleveland, Ohio.

As a little boy, we as a family traveled to Cleveland to visit family and friends. On one of these trips, we took Route US 2, which would connect us to Lake Avenue. Traveling down Lake Ave., which is on the west side of Cleveland, Mom began to point out Lake Avenue School, where she attended. She also pointed out several mansions where she had lived as a child with her mother who did domestic work there.

It was during this conversation that she said the actress, Ethel Waters had been visiting one of her friends who were the homeowners. While there, Ms. Waters met and became acquainted with Mother and Grandmother Mary Lou. She immediately developed a keen attentiveness to my Mother. Ethel Waters saw how gifted mother was and she begged Grandmother Mary Lou to let her adopt Mom and take her back to Hollywood.

There, Ethel Waters could give Mary Lou the proper and superior education, as well as the cultural training that was needed. Grandmother Mary Lou was adamant and refused to let her namesake, Mary Louise go with Ms. Waters.

Even despite Grandmother Mary Lou's refusal to agree with Ethel Waters' proposition, my Mother's time and growing up with my Grandmother Mary Lou was so very special. She loved her so very much."

This is an *original handbill* from the theatrical play, *"Cabin in the Sky"*, starring, Ethel Waters. She was known for her *standards of excellence on the stage.*

This is a June 12, 1971 press photo of Billy Graham, Ethel Waters and Ruth Graham arriving at the White House for Tricia Nixon's Wedding.

During this timeframe Ethel Waters was well known for singing one of her signature hymns, "His Eye is on the Sparrow" on the national Billy Graham televised crusades.

I was always fascinated watching those performances as my Mother reminded me of her very own encounter with Ethel Waters. (Photo Source: Personal EBay Purchase)

The way that Mother initially *(in 1970)* explained it to me, *(many years before her 2013 conversation with Hubert),* was that Miss Waters saw something special in her and she wanted to see it developed with her monetary means and national influence. However, the offer from Ethel Waters was never even a consideration for Mary Louise.

Because of her own desires to see Mary Lou go to Oakwood College, Mary Louise wanted to see her promised daughter bloom beyond the blessings that had come from her aging, worn and tired domestic hands. She wanted so much more for Mary Lou than she had obtained in her own life. Grandmother Mary Lou's dreams for her namesake involved a Christian Education. She wanted the best for Mary Lou, but more than anything, Mary Louise wanted God's blessing upon Mary Lou's life.

Whatever brilliance and natural talent that Ethel Waters had seen in Mary Lou surely ended up blooming beyond many blessings. Mary Lou was in her National Honor Society in high school, and when Langston Hughes came to speak at Central High for the National Honor Society Induction, he autographed the back of Mary Lou's Honor Society Membership Card. Central High School was a fine preparatory experience not only for Mary Lou's collegiate days, but also for the foundational life skills that would form her future experiences.

On the above left, is a photo of Ethel Waters life story. Next to it is a photo of her album, His Eye is on the Sparrow. For further information, visit the following you tube link to view the 1967 Mike Douglas interview with Ethel Waters. https://youtu.be/za8QEqXn4_0

*(See page 277 & 278 for additional information)

This is Mary Lou's Central High School, Senior Year Photo. (Spring of 1943) Mary Lou was 17 years old when she graduated from Central High School. At 17, Mary Louise Battle was ready to face the world to fulfill her dreams. As a National Honor Society Graduate, Mary Lou's Mindset was already determined with courage and faith in God's Will.

After her high school graduation in 1943, Mary Lou decided to work at the *Stone Knitting Mill* in Cleveland. She worked hard for two years to save up money for her college fees. While doing this, Mary Lou also helped Mary Louise in some of the homes where she was serving wealthy and privileged families.

Experiencing the bitter cup of racism from some "Midwestern Mindsets" that subtly projected indifference toward Negroes, brought a preparation for Mary Lou's college days. There she would face some of the boldest bigotry from a harsher Alabama Mentality, that made absolutely no apology for its' commitment to ignorant intolerance.

Later days down the road would show how Mary Lou's determination and resilience was all a necessary process of blooming. When she faced the crossing of the *Mason Dixon Line* and traveled back into *"Jim Crow Counties"*, within Kentucky, where she had been born, then, her deepest inner strength was again tested.

She had to remain silent in the face of racism's ridicule, as she and her classmates from Cleveland moved to sit behind the coal cars when they got to Cincinnati. My Mother never forgot the memories of riding in those segregated seats behind those sooty coal cars. She spoke of just how dusty her clothes would be by the end of the seven-hour journey to Huntsville, Alabama. Once on the College Campus of Oakwood, after the segregated ride, there was an immediate need to be refreshed, redressed and relieved from all that coal dust.

However, the ridicule of racism's sting never was too far away whenever Mary Lou made trips to town to purchase necessary items. The store clerks were quick to greet Mary Lou with an abrupt,*"**What do you want gal"**,* rather than the courteous, ***"May I help you?"***, that those exact same store clerks eagerly gave the Caucasian customers. What should have been a pleasant shopping experience was wrapped in the southern customs of racial bigotry and American inequalities. Being silent was the only *"safe choice"* that an African American could make in that era, in order to be free from any repercussions.

Those years of blooming brought a mindset to Mary Lou that could not be shaken. Mary Lou's Mindset was being shaped and sharpened by life experiences of toil, trial and triumph. Being the only child of Mary Louise, helped Mary Lou in the fact that she became her own advocate in adversity and her own rule of thumb to measure herself by without living with any siblings. Through days of being alone, whenever Mary Louise worked without her, Mary Lou took time to educate herself through reading and music. Those independent moments of solace gave her the opportunity to broaden the foundation of her own ideals.

Growing up between two Mothers also gave Mary Lou many opportunities of gaining insights into the talents of two strong women who had learned the value of self-reliance and independence regardless of circumstance. These lessons of resilience and courage from both Mothers were like two pillars of power that could never be moved. Thus the Mindset of Mary Lou propelled beyond blessings, because it was forged within the mentorship of two strong minded women who had learned to persevere, pray and progress, even in the worst of times.

King James Bible

Therefore, shall a man leave his father and his mother, and shall cleave unto his wife: and they shall be one flesh.

Genesis 2:24

King James Bible

Lo, children are a heritage of the LORD: and the fruit of the womb is his reward.

Psalm 127:3

CHAPTER 3
Baby Blessings

"Transitions from an Engaged Collegiate to a Wife and Mother"

Brand new blooms arrived in Mary Lou's life when the Spring of 1945 came. It was as though nature was proclaiming that new growth not only would grace the earth, but new growth would also develop within the life of a young lady who was entering the Spring of her amazing womanhood. Nothing ever seemed ordinary in our Mother's life. For the most part, her life experiences did not fit "the norm". Mary Lou was living "outside of the proverbial box" before she ever left her Mother's womb, because of the promise that Pearl made to Mary Louise.

For every rainbow in Mary Lou's life, there was definite rainfall and at times, there were great thunderstorms. Much of the strength of "Mary Lou's Mindset" had come from daily observations of her namesake, Mary Louise. She had been named after and given to a woman of God's own order. Mary Louise was not just a "praying woman", but over everything else, Mary Louise was a "practicing woman", who lived her religion every time she took a breath. In all of the times that we went to visit her in Cleveland, I cannot ever remember her getting angry.

She was a woman of amazing peace and great love. How she could be so graceful after all that she had endured is still a wonder. And even when the husband that she so beloved abandoned her and Mary Lou, this woman demonstrated the truth about her faith in God. She did not despair, complain or become bitter. Against all odds, Mary Louise persistently prayed and persistently persevered. Her faith was her fortune because she carried a wealth of dignity, determination and duty in the details of her daily agendas.

Our Grandmother, Mary Louise, was truly noble in most every sense of the word. If one should consider that her greatest offense was woven in the deceitful way that she and Pearl schemed in order to give her the joys of Motherhood, then one must also realize the weight that Mary Louise carried for partaking in that offense. For the rest of her entire lifetime, after taking baby Mary Lou home, Mary Louise had to psychologically pay for her contribution of bringing unnecessary discord within the lives of Pearl and Joel's family. Every time she came in contact with the Battle family, she had to wear the label of being "the one who took Joel's daughter".

Although I can't remember anyone ever saying one bad thing about "Grandma Mary Lou", I can remember some of the "silent stares" that one of my Grandfather Joel's sisters gave her at a family reunion. If a picture is worth a thousand words, then that look which came from my Great Aunt that day, was hollering close to ten thousand words.

Life has its own way of applying retribution for the unnecessary acts of our impulsive and intentional deeds. A moment of selfishness can bring unbelievable consequences that remain perpetual. But before we cast judgment and make ourselves a judge and a jury on Mary Louise, we must ask ourselves, who do we know that has not ever been selfish? Who can wear that lofty label of "Unselfish

Lifetime Achiever"?

Of course Mary Louise was incorrect to align herself with Pearl's plot, especially with having done so without Joel's knowledge. Yet, one cannot dismiss the fact that her greatest offense was truly linked to one of her deepest desires..., "Motherhood".

But was the object of her affection worth the consequential conflicts that she carried with her for the rest of her life?

Only God can fully know the answer to that question. What is known is that Mary Louise gave all that she had to daily show her steadfast love to Mary Lou. If she had been rich with money and material items, then Mary Lou could have been spoiled beyond rotten. But the priceless gifts of goodness, kindness, loyalty, respect and honor, totally out measured any single, vain, or earthly treasure.

The unmatched beauty of "Grandmother Mary Lou's heart", gave precedence over any superficial beauty standard in this entire world. Neither the depth of her beautiful dark chocolate skin, the coarseness of her overworked hands, the simplicity of her features, nor the meekness of her mind could lessen her inner beauty or render her ordinary, in my mind. She was a heroine with an angelic presence. The aura of her heart superseded everything physical about her.

As clean and as orderly as she kept her home, she also kept a pristine heart. She was slow to speak words but quick to share love. ***That is what made Grandmother Mary Lou one of the most beautiful women that I have ever known.*** She was like the Proverbs 31 Woman, *"priceless and beyond beauty"*. After over six decades of living, I cannot say that I have ever known any individual as meek and intentionally observant as she was. Her heart was a place of peace and a palace of purity. Loving God and loyalty to Him was the trend for her life's obedience.

If one sentence depicted her, it could be the one found in the book of Isaiah 30:5 which says,

"In quietness and confidence shall be your strength."

This is a photo of Hazel, Mary Lou's second oldest sister on the far left. Mary Louise Washington - Battle, who Mary Lou called "Little Mama" is standing in the middle. My Mother, Mary Lou is on the right end in the striped dress. This was taken in 1964 at my Uncle Felix Battle's home in Cleveland. This picture shows how the years of hard work had left their evidence on Grandmother Mary Lou's hands. Decades of domestic labor had shown the constant toil that Mary Louise had experienced. Yet those difficulties could not break down or take away her beautiful smile and stellar spirit. Neither could the toils of life take away her tremendous faith in God.

Her favorite hymn , "Abide With Me", was sung at Mary Louise's funeral which was held at the Glenville SDA Church in Cleveland. Listen to the hymn in the link https://youtu.be/NTT5HGSaO-Y?si=PXQrOJSgygzdEPae

I truly believe that Mary Lou's strength was so great because Mary Louise's strength had been even greater. That's what influenced Mary Lou's womanhood the most. Her wonderful opportunity to be graced with the witness of such strong standards of character, enabled Mary Lou to stand in the same strength that had shaped her spirit.

With that kind of foundational fortitude, it is no wonder why a handsome gentleman from Toledo, Ohio came to Cleveland to seek Mary Lou out. He was well groomed, well dressed and keenly attentive to the actions of this beautiful, poised and intelligent young woman who made 19 look like perfection.

As Mary Lou stood in the front of the church giving her Sabbath School Secretary's Report on that bright Saturday morning, that day suddenly became even brighter for Hugh Washington. He had heard a glowing report about Mary Lou from one of his former quartet members.

Hugh decided that he should take a drive to Cleveland after listening to those angelic and awesome reviews from his quartet associate, Leroy Hemingway. Hugh was born in 1919 which made him six years older than Mary Lou.

This is the portrait that Hugh gave to Mary Lou before she left Cleveland to attend Oakwood College.

By being 25 at the time, Hugh was ready to find a wife and settle down to enjoy his own family. Leroy Hemingway made it so very simple for Hugh by sharing his braggadocious story of how he planned to go back home to Cleveland and find Mary Lou one day. That's why one should always be careful how they share their dreams and with whom they share them. Loyalty is not always exercised, especially when someone is ready to find a prospective wife.

Some may view Hugh as being "a dream snatcher", however, Mary Lou was not engaged to anyone. She was just coming into the prime of her life. Although Mary Lou was a beautiful woman to behold, she was still *"untouched"* as the old folks used to say. Virginity was the crown that Mary Louise had placed upon her promised daughter.

My Mother's exact words are forever etched in my mind, because she shared Grandma Mary Lou's firm opinion about her virginity with me. My Mother said,

"Mama always told me that I had to be careful about everything that I did because if I ever got pregnant or in any kind of trouble, the Battle families would blame her."

Deeper than that counsel was the fact that Mary Lou had sisters who were not virgins and that had gotten pregnant before marriage. Sadly, one of her sisters had been forced by Pearl to have an illegal abortion and almost bled to death because of the way she was medically abused. Because of the abortion, that sister was never able to have any children. Unfortunately, she had been robbed of ever becoming a mother because of her own Mother's dictates.

In addition, Pearl had been part of a deliberate scheme in which one of her other older daughters had gotten pregnant before marriage and had been forced to give her child away to one of Pearl's sisters to raise. Pearl allowed her own grandchild to be taken from his birth mother, while growing up with so many psychological shadows of wondering who his real mother was. She lived with these deliberately chosen actions, against her very own daughters, as though she had never done anything offensive towards them. Yet, as strongly as Pearl had violated the lives of those two daughters to keep their unwed pregnancies away from her household, she seemingly did nothing to help repair the devastation from those losses that her daughters had experienced. She kept these violations as secret as she could. It was as though they were protected as much as if they were her costly, hidden treasures.

Because of those dark realities, Mary Lou heeded the serious and firm guidance of Mary Louise. I don't think that Mary Lou would have purposely done anything to bring any form of sorrow, shame or scandal to her Mother, Mary Louise. On the other side of that ironic coin, Mary Lou wanted the favour, affirmation and pride from both Pearl and Joel, her birth parents. She did not want them to be disappointed either.

With three parents to please, as well as a host of family members, Mary Lou was held to a standard well above her siblings and peers. In addition, there were also the biblical standards that held her accountable to the denominational beliefs that she was raised to believe. Disregarding any of those levels would be as disowning who she was at her core. Because she was deeply attached to the church leadership roles and regular mentoring activities that she was involved with, morality was paramount in all of her decisions.

Mary Lou is photographed as a Pathfinder Guide at Cleveland 31st. and Cedar S.D.A. Church. (She is standing in the second row, standing directly behind seated children and is the second person going from left to right.) Catherine Battle, Mary Lou's baby sister is seated first on the left of the front row. Cecil Coes is seated second from Catherine. Two seats from Cecil is Evangelist William Scales at a young age. Elder Scales sings in 1956 Oakwood's Cathedral Quartet. Listen to the link.

https://youtu.be/X5pdT6gTG_Q?si=8PJj6FlmWzGfj-4J

Years later, Cecil Coes would be introduced to his future wife, Dorothy Barnes from Toledo, because of Mary Lou's matchmaking. The last picture to the right, shows Mary Lou many years later as a Pathfinder Master Guide.

Hugh Washington would not be the temptation to change her mindset. Although older and well-seasoned about the matters of life, Hugh knew, after taking only *one day* to observe Mary Lou, that she was a woman of integrity and quality. That day he found that the sum of Leroy's description was totally accurate. With the boldness of a skilled professional charmer, Hugh approached Mary Lou with great anticipation. However, being the gentleman that he had been raised to be, Hugh received all of the addresses from all of the single ladies that approached him that day after the church service.

Mary Lou did not follow behind him to form a conversation. Neither did she approach him to give him her address. Hugh sought her out and remarked, *"I didn't get your address."*

Mary Lou confidently responded by saying, *"I don't know why you want it because you're not going to use it."* Hugh then gave an instant rebuttal with the challenge,

"Give it to me and I'll show you something different."

My Mother said that she gave Hugh the address, even though she did not really believe that he would actually write her a letter. But what Mary Lou truly did not know at that time was that Hugh Washington was on a mission and that mission was called, *"Marrying Mary Lou."*

Before the end of the incoming week, Hugh had sent Mary Lou the very first of his many letters. That day began the first of many trips which Hugh made driving his bright, shiny 1943 Chevy, with a clean all leather interior, from Toledo to Cleveland to spend time with his sweetheart, Mary Lou.

When the summer of 1945 ended, and before Mary Lou left Cleveland to attend college, Hugh Washington presented Mary Lou with an "engagement watch" which was the custom of their religion at that time.

This is the photo that my Mother gave to my Father in 1944. She was working at Cleveland's Stone Knitting Mill to earn money for her college tuition to attend Oakwood. Mary Lou was 19 years old.

Hugh was not willing to forfeit the woman of his heart. Neither was Hugh going to find himself disappointed as Leroy was going to be when he learned of the news about Hugh and Mary Lou's future marriage. To allow Mary Lou every advantage of fulfilling her educational goals, Hugh regularly sent money to Mary Lou to help with her tuition payments. He told her that he had no problem with her casually dating other young men who were her friends or classmates, because Hugh knew that when Mary Lou finished school and returned to Ohio, they would be married.

Mary Lou is standing beside her classmates on the campus of Oakwood in 1945 or 46. This photo is in the actual 1946 Oakwood yearbook. Turner Battle III, the artist who designed the Oakwood University Seal, was also the Art Editor of that Historic 1946 Oakwood Yearbook. It was the very first yearbook that Oakwood ever had. Ironically, Turner is Mary Lou's first cousin. His father Turner Battle II was the brother of Pearl Battle, Mary Lou's birth Mother. In the next photo, they are pictured together in later years at an Oakwood University Alumni.

Mary Lou is happily standing in the middle of her two brilliant cousins,
Dr. Douglas Chandler on the left, in the white jacket and Dr. Turner Battle III,
on the right, in the blue jacket. According to Cousin Turner, this picture was
taken during Oakwood Alumni Weekend 2000.

Dr. Turner Battle III is the original designer and creator of the Oakwood
University Seal and also the Art Designer of the 1946 Oakwood College 50th.
Anniversary Yearbook. As one of the United Negro College Fund Vice Presidents,
Cousin Turner made sure Oakwood University received numerous funding during
his UNCF (United Negro College Fund) appointments.

Mary Lou always wanted to see her first cousin, Turner honored publicly and
appropriately by the "Administrators" at Oakwood. However, she went to her grave
in 2013 never having witnessed that desire. The Alumni Association President,
under the leadership of Mrs. Chlora Jones did recognize Cousin Turner with a
plaque (that he had Mary Lou receive in his absence) during her time as a Dean.
Though much appreciated, it was the Administration that still had not honored Dr.
Battle who was the one that is responsible for the official seal that represents the
Oakwood University Business worldwide.

She always remarked at every Oakwood Commencement how she felt it was not correct that Turner had been overlooked concerning his design of the Official Oakwood Seal. As she saw the University Seal annually on every Commencement Program Booklet from 1987 through 2007 (during her years of serving at Oakwood) she never failed to speak about how Turner should have been "appropriately honored".

Not only had he created the Oakwood Seal and Oakwood's 1946 50th. Anniversary Yearbook, but Cousin Turner had also taught as an Art Instructor for Oakwood while he was still a student there.

Mary Lou always believed that a person was due their rightful respect and recognition for a job well done. This is why she held such a firm position about her Cousin Turner being appropriately and administratively honored. Ironically even now in 2024, almost 11 years after my Mother's Death, Cousin Turner has still not been recognized for those contributions. At this time of editing, 2024, He is now 98 years of age.

This is a black and white picture of the official Oakwood University Seal that Turner Battle, III designed while a student at Oakwood College in the 1940's. When displayed in color, it is seen with the traditional royal blue and gold university colors.

Turner   Maurice   Mary lou

This picture shows a part of the childhood memories that Mary Lou had when she spent time with her cousins Turner and Maurice Battle. *See pages 259 & 260 They were the nephews of her birth Mother, Pearl and the sons of Pearl's brother, Turner Battle, II. See pages 259, 260 & 261 for more information.

This picture is from the 1946 Oakwood College 50th Anniversary Yearbook. It shows Mary Lou's cousin, Turner Battle III, (yearbook art editor) teaching one of his college art classes. Turner was an art instructor while he and Mary Lou were in college attending Oakwood. Cousin Turner is on the very far right guiding his students.

Dear Michelle,

I just learned that your mother passed away. My feelings are with you during this time of sorrow.

My thoughts of her go back to the 1920s when we were three and four years old. My parents purchased a home in Oberlin, OH. Often your mother, Aunt Pearline, and Uncle Joel came down from Cleveland to visit us. Everyone including my parents and I piled into our car and my Dad drove us up to Lake Erie where your mother and I played in the sand. On one occasion, we wandered away down the beach. My Dad found us some distance away talking to strangers. Everyone was relieved when he brought us back unharmed. Mary Lou was my first playmate. We found ourselves together again when I left Andrews University in 1945 to stay at Aunt Pearline's home after which we found ourselves again together as students at Oakwood College in 1947. I have pleasant thoughts of our relationship through the years. They will remain with me for the rest of my life. She was a wonderful cousin whom I loved.

In closing, please accept my heartfelt sympathy for the loss of your mother who was a respectable, kind, and fine mother, cousin, and friend whom we all loved. I join our family members and her many friends who are comforting and praying for you and the family.

During this time of sorrow, I pray each of you will receive a Special Blessing.

Love, your cousin,

Turner

(Turner C. Battle III)

This is the letter of sympathy that Cousin Turner emailed me on August 23, 2013.

According to my Mother, Hugh never worried about her breaking her promise to marry him. He was confident that Mary Lou was a woman of her worth and her word. And as she said in her very own words,

"Your Father was willing to wait. He did not mind waiting for me to go to school because he knew that I was serious about my education and that those were the only conditions that I would agree to."

However, Hugh was deeply concerned that one of Mary Lou's Oakwood admirers would influence her to reconsider and call off her engagement to him if possible.

Hugh knew that Mary Lou was a woman of great integrity and great value.

This is one of my absolutely favorite pictures of my parents. It was taken during the time of their engagement when they were both a part of their friends' wedding party in Cleveland. How truly content both Mary Lou and Hugh look with each other in this photograph.

In June of 1947, Mary Lou graduated with her Associate Degree in Business from the only Seventh-day Adventist University that originated as an 1896 African American Trade School and still remains among our "*Historical Black Colleges and Universities*" (HBCU) in America.

Upon returning to Cleveland within the same month, Mary Lou fulfilled her promise and married Hugh. Originally Mary Lou had planned to complete her 4 years and receive her Bachelor's Degree in Business. Standing between the intermittent intervals of Hugh's constant urging to her to marry and the continual need to meet college payments, Mary Lou decided to modify her initial plans.

By the following year, November of 1948, Mary Lou would become a Mother herself. She and Hugh happily embraced their first of three babies. In 1948, Hubert Dale Washington was born on November 19. What a memorable Thanksgiving Hugh and Mary Lou had during that second Thanksgiving of their marriage.

Hubert is around 1 years old in this picture. Mary Lou designed and made his pants and matching cap.

However, everything was not all joyful concerning the birth of Mary Lou and Hugh's first child. After this first birthing process came immediate and deep shock. When a woman has carried a baby for 9 months, then pushes through the stages of delivery to bring her child out of the birth chamber, holding her newborn baby is usually her greatest joy. In the Fall of November, 1948, Mary Lou found herself within the ecstasy of such joy, until her Doctor informed her of some devastating news.

The overshadowing news that Mary Lou's Doctor brought her could have wounded and crushed her beyond any limits of rebounding, had it not been for her mindset of spiritual faith. This was her very first pregnancy and childbirth.She and Hugh had faithfully prayed for a son at every meal throughout Mary Lou's pregnancy. What a wonderful answer to their petitions, when God answered their faithful prayers with their baby boy, Hubert.

Nothing could have been more wonderful at this stage of their newlywed lives. They were truly happy about God's blessing of a new son until the truth was revealed from Dr. Levin, Mary Lou's OBGYN. When Dr. Levin entered Mary Lou's room after her delivery, he was faced with bearing bad news to her about baby Hubert.

Hubert was born with all 10 fingers and all ten toes. Born prematurely and at a little over 5 pounds, Hubert had other issues that were troubling all by themselves. He was perfectly innocent, yet the revealer of the devastating news that was meant to come forth and could no longer be withheld.

As Dr. Levin approached Mary Lou, he was direct and yet professionally concerned. He had known Mary Lou to be a wonderful patient with integrity, goodness and grace. But despite his high regard for a good patient, he had to deliver the truth to Mary Lou, no matter how uncomfortably sad it may have been. With his stoic professionalism, Dr. Levin proceeded to tell Mary Lou that the little tiny bumps on Hubert's body were the result of a sexual venereal disease. This is the account that my Mother shared with me concerning the incident:

"When Dr. Levin came into my room and informed me that Hubert was broken out with tiny bumps due to a venereal disease, I was so embarrassed. I knew that it could have only come from your father having sexual indiscretions because Hugh was the only man that I had ever had sexual relations with. Can you imagine how hurt I was and also angered and embarrassed to see Doctor Levin looking at me after sharing such information? I wondered if he thought I was a dirty, loose woman and an unfaithful wife. As I laid in that hospital bed and thought about it all, I also felt a lot of anger toward your Father's unfaithfulness and sexual indiscretions. All I could think about was how I had been a virgin when I married your Father. I had

kept my commitment to marry him before leaving to attend Oakwood College. My faithfulness to your father had started long before I ever married him. There were so many other young men who had shown serious interest in dating me who were my college classmates. They were bold about their intentions. One of them even boldly told me,

"Hugh is there, (in Ohio) I am here. (at Oakwood)"

Hugh is seen here as one of the wedding participants for Mary Lou's Cleveland friends.

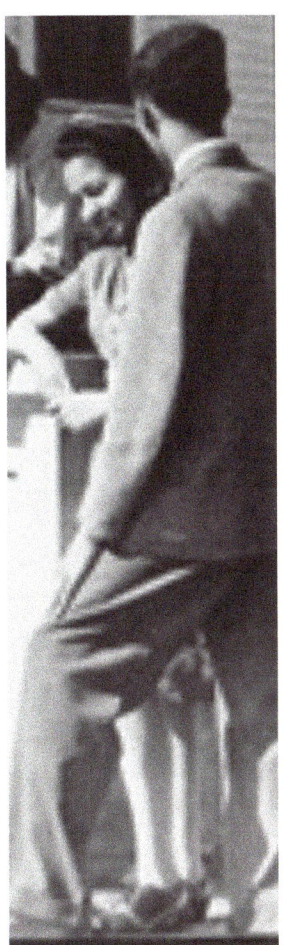

This picture is of Mary Lou as a student at Oakwood College between 1945-47. She is standing on the campus at the historic water fountain. The last photo shows Mary Lou listening to a fellow classmate during her first year at Oakwood.

*"I thought about the fact that your father had pressured me to marry him with a 2-year associate degree, when it was my dream of completing my 4-year business degree. I had altered my dreams because of your Father's wishes. I felt betrayed by the man that I had faithfully kept my promises to. While lying in bed at Toledo's Riverside Hospital, I seriously considered taking Hubert and leaving your Father. That was not an easy time for me because I knew Hugh had to have been unfaithful **after** our wedding, since the State of Ohio required a blood test before marriage. There had been no evidence of any sexual diseases from those premarital blood tests. You can never imagine how this experience touched my life. I really did not want to stay in the marriage with your Father."*

It was my Mother's Mindset of extreme faith in God that kept her through this unsettling and horrific experience. She had done nothing wrong yet she had been wronged by the man with whom she had vowed to love, honor and cherish. How could she stay with such a man who had ignored those same matrimonial vows while dishonoring her? How could she handle leaving her precious little baby boy in the hospital for a few extra days, because of need for treatment and medical care due to a condition caused by Hugh's infidelity? Only a mindset anchored to God's Promises brought Mary Lou's thinking to a higher plateau of spiritual soundness. A level of loving and trusting in God was the greater power surrounding Mary Lou in her time of troubling distress.

For those of you who may be going through similar experiences as that which my Mother went through, whether you are a woman or man facing marital infidelity, please know that you can overcome your levels of scorn. It is no longer 1948. Although biblically, Mary Lou had every spiritual freedom to divorce Hugh with biblical cause, she chose to stay in her marriage. Regardless of what was within her rights of having biblical grounds for divorcing my father, my Mother chose to go spiritually high when my father chose to go morally low.

Now in 2024, as I am editing this book, some of you may need to move forward with a freedom that only a biblically based divorce can bring. If that is your case, do not allow the judgmental bondage of others to interfere with what God's Words of deliverance may be for you. If God has given us a clear and sound way of marital divorcement through His Word, who then can point any finger to those who have the spiritual right to walk away from marital disrespect, martial violations and adulterous bondage?

As my Mother lived with her choices of remaining married to my Father, she also lived with thoughts of how her life may have been so entirely different if she had divorced him and moved forward. Mary Lou knew that with her steadfast faith, tenacity and perseverance, she could have easily gone back to school and completed her other two years of college, in order to receive her four-year degree. She would have had a totally different life, had she chosen to divorce.

A divorce from my Father would have also meant that my sister, Marla and I would have not been born. My Mother truly honored her vows of "for better or worse...until death we do part". Mary Lou set her mind to choose what most individuals would not have chosen. She chose to endure a journey that was not easy from the very foundational days of her marriage.

By the time my Mother decided that it was okay to share the hospital story surrounding Hubert's birth, I was well into my twenties. It shattered a lot of "*the stained glass window ideas*" that I had always believed about my Father. As a

Daddy's Girl, my thoughts had to make a transition into the truth if I was going to be honest about the reality about my Father. Because he had been dead since my 14th year of life, I could not have the privilege of confronting my Dad. That was a good thing, because I don't know what that conversation may have been like had my Father been alive to hear my concerns about his choice to dishonor my Mother with marital infidelity.

The Bible reminds us that,

"We all have sinned and fallen short of the glory of God." Romans 3:23

It also lets us know we are all on the same level when it comes to our spiritual status. It is because of that reason that *none of us* can ever point a finger at anyone. Yet, as a daughter, there would have been a defending spirit that would have not been quiet on behalf of my Mother's sake. We never, ever *fully* know what secrets our parents have withheld from us, even in our adulthoods, in order to protect our peace of mind.

As my senior citizen womanhood now reflects the journey of my Mother, I must honor my Mother's memory from a whole new perspective. Having been by her cancerous bedside as she drew her last breaths boldly smiling, at the age of 88, what I now can easily see is just how truly deep her mindset was. Yes, our Mother, the Mother of Hubert, Marla and Michelle was anchored in the Lord. She was a Mother who had lived with a Golden and a Godly Mindset. She had ignored some of her own inner conflicts to propel herself past the decision of divorce.

Her issues of abandonment from her childhood had to have revisited her during the timeframe of learning Hugh's unfaithfulness. ***Regardless of how one may label or view marital infidelity and adultery, it is the psychological, physical and spiritual abandonment of choosing to ignore the marriage vows to your spouse while choosing to be unfaithful with someone who is not a part of the sacred matrimonial commitment.***

Although those marital indiscretions may be ever so secretively private and only known by God, they are still *in violation of Heaven's Order*s when governed by the holy standards of God's Word which says,

"What therefore God has joined together, let not man put asunder." Matthew 19:6

Despite the deep darkness of Hugh's indiscretion, Mary Lou remained true to what was within her heart. Choosing to take *an unguaranteed journey*, she looked beyond the "for worse" and focused on the "for better" part of her marriage vows.

In the photo above, Hubert is standing with his matching cap and coat not far from Mary Lou. Always the protective Mother, Mary Lou always kept a close eye on her firstborn child. She is standing next to Hugh surrounded by the Bethel SDA Church Members who were breaking ground for the building of their first church. It was located at the corner of Elizabeth and Vance Street in the City Park Neighborhood of Toledo, Ohio. First Elder Charles Wilson (with hat in hand and on shovel) and Pastor James Thomas hold shovel. Not far away is Elder Harry Dobbins, Sr. on the far left, front row.

As beautiful as Mary Lou is pristinely standing as a supportive wife, she mirrored this kind of loyalty to Hugh throughout their years of marriage. Never did any of those church members ever have any knowledge of Hugh's indiscretion and unfaithfulness that took place before Hubert's birth. Mary Lou's Mindset forged a foundational platform to rise above Hugh's weakness and reach beyond his momentary selfishness.

What kind of determination could propel her to make such a firm decision and stay committed to that decision? This is far past any thoughts that my imagination can ever create or even find. Harbored within the deepest corners of Mary Lou's Mindset was a staying power of spirituality that only God could have given her. With her own human strength, she could not have made the choice to forgive Hugh nor even think about remaining with him as his lifelong spouse. The biblical love that 1 Corinthians 13 defines is the standard of love that Mary Lou gave to Hugh.

Her choice was as the standard defines in verse 5 of Corinthians 13, when it says, "seeketh not her own". Had Mary Lou used a human standard of love that so often seeks selfishness, she would have chosen as Hugh had done. Had that been her choice, then their marriage would have ended on the day Hubert was born. Mary Lou's **one choice,** prompted by God's Word, was the spiritual compass that directed her through her marital storm.

Almost a decade had passed. In 1956, Mary Lou and Hugh's second baby was born. After eight years of giving only one child attention, Marla Lynne took her place for attention in the world with no stones left unturned. My Mother shared her account of how abruptly Marla's delivery began.

She recalled,

"By the time your Father got me to the hospital, Marla's little feet were sticking out. Because my regular Doctor was away, an intern had to perform the delivery. Everyone was nervous as they hollered out that the baby was breech."

Breech births were a greater risk in those days as compared to the knowledge that Doctors now have. Although there are still factors of risk with the delivery of breech births, it is nothing like it was over 60 years ago. Yet even within that momentum of possible loss, "Mary Lou's Mindset" was focused more on God's faithfulness to the prayers that she and Hugh had prayed.

Even before Hubert was born, Hugh and Mary Lou prayed this prayer at each meal,

"Thank you Lord for the food and for the son that you will give us."

So before Marla was born, the prayer before each meal was changed to,

"Thank you Lord for the food and for the daughter that you will give us."

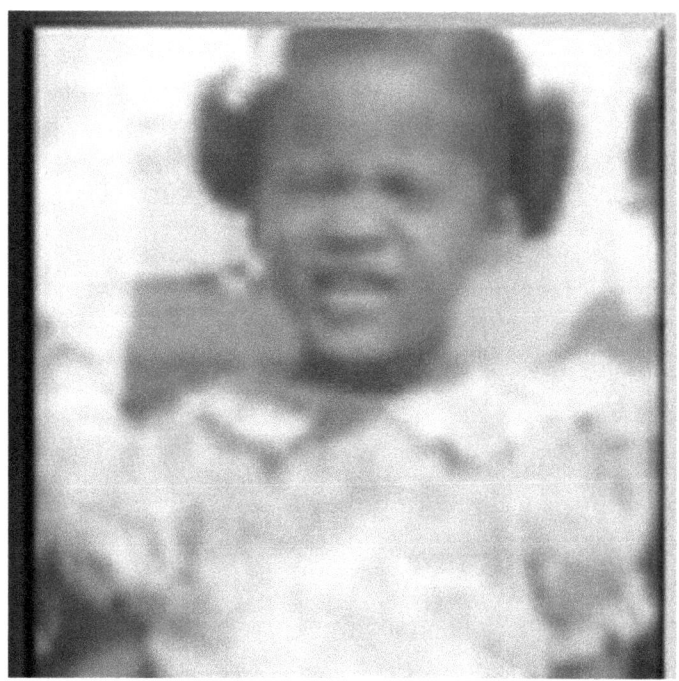

Pictured above is Marla around the time that she was praying for a sister.

So after Marla was safely born, Mary Lou felt that her child bearing days were complete. She had given Hugh the desired son which most fathers want so that their family name can continue. Now by having a baby girl, Mary Lou felt that she had the best example of a model family.

Too bad that Marla did not agree. She prayed to God for a little sister and God answered Marla's prayers. In 1960, I was born and given the name Michelle Linda.

This photo is of my Father, Hugh Washington and I in the backyard of our Clay Avenue family home. I was around one-year-old.

Once again, 4 years later, Mary Lou found herself embracing a brand new baby. Once again God had answered the mealtime prayer of praise that said,

"Thank you Lord for the food and for the daughter that you will give us."

Being the Mother of three children in 1960 was no easy task especially when one considers the gaps between our births. Hubert was 8 years old when Marla was born and he was 12 years old when I was born. Marla was 4 when I was born. My Mother often said that she didn't plan it quite that way. However, it worked out when it came to paying for our tuition to receive a Christian Education.

Mary Lou's third pregnancy was not one she had planned or wanted. Yes, she loved all of her children however, the reality of the marital turbulence that she had experienced with Hugh was not anything that could be erased. Though forgiveness had been given to Hugh, how deeply Mary Lou had to depend upon the Characteristics of God's Mercy and Grace, when memories resurfaced surrounding Hugh's infidelity before Hubert's birth.

It is easy for me to understand why my Mother was not placing a third child upon her agenda. For this reason, she often referred to me as "my bonus baby". On the evening of my birth, my Father told Mary Lou, "I don't know why you don't want to have any more children, when you have such beautiful babies."

Left to right is Hubert, Marla and I standing next to the peach trees in our yard on Clay Avenue. This was taken in 1963. Though blurry, this shows some acreage of the land behind us, as well as the gaps in our ages Hubert 15, Marla 7, and I was 3.

My Mother shared so many of her inner thoughts with me throughout the years. I believe it was because I was the one who was quick to ask detailed questions about the family history. I didn't stop at only asking her questions, but also her older sister, Hazel, who was my favorite aunt.

I could ask Aunt Hazel just about anything and about everything, I knew that she would tell me "the absolute truth." This was a great blessing to my life because it enabled me to have a greater understanding about Grandmother Pearl, Grandmother Mary Lou and most of all, my Mother.

My Mother could be complicated because her life had been complicated. She was not always easy to understand or communicate with because she had not had an easy or normal upbringing. The controversial issues between her parents were at the very core of her inner thoughts. Being caught in the middle between Joel and Pearl's indifferences, Mary Lou could not be near a place of joyful pleasantries.

There within the parental circles of their confusion, she was deficient of receiving a sufficient amount of affirming feelings for a young child's experiences. Pearl was living with regrets and Joel was living with a sense of betrayal, disgust and hurt regarding the entire situation concerning little Mary Lou.

There wasn't an open platform to discuss those kinds of issues back in that day. So much was left unspoken and placed "on mute". Within that time frame, children definitely were frequently raised to be "seen and not heard."

 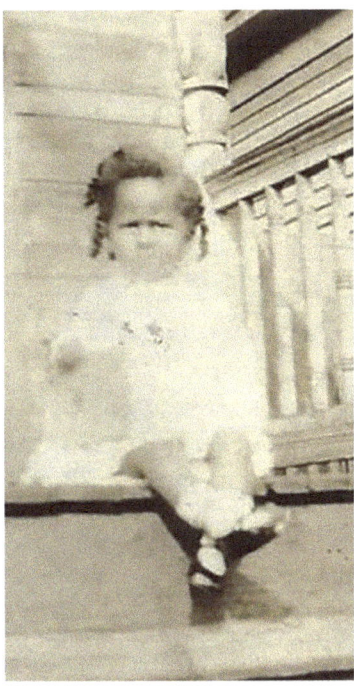

Mary Lou is around 3 years old. Her expression shows how serious she was even at a young age. She has a firm grip on the book in her right hand.

There was definitely turmoil surrounding young Mary Lou and she felt the struggle between her parents. Add to that the issues that stood between Mary Louise and Wright. Who could deny just how much uneasiness surrounded Mary Lou within both environments? These areas of negative adult relationships were issues that were certainly unpleasant and difficult for Mary Lou to witness. Although they were not issues that she had created, somewhere, within her young mind, she felt sorry about partially being the reason that the differences existed.

That kind of sorrow and guilt was one that Mary Lou carried within the depths of her soul as she grew up. I can remember her saying that she felt as though her parents' marital problems and separation were largely due to her being given away. Even in her adulthood, she had not worked through many of the issues that were still confronting her psychologically and disturbing her spirit. What I do now know is that my Mother pushed back and kept so many things inside of herself, because of the Mother that she was striving to be. She was determined not to make the same mistakes that Pearl and Mary Louise had made. Yet, with all of the determination in the entire world, Mary Lou could never be a perfect Mother in an imperfect world.

However, her constant need to prove that she could rise above her childhood shadows, inwardly motivated her to strive to be the very best Mother that she could be. She felt blessed to have her children and Mary Lou wanted in every way to be a blessing to their lives. Her mindset was unbelievably determined regarding the wellbeing of her own children. Not in any way, had Mary Lou ever intended to watch her children repeat her experiences of witnessing parental and marital discord or unhappiness.

The blessings of having a baby and becoming a Mother, had now reached the life of one whose birth arrangements had caused so much confusion. Now Mary Lou could focus on proving what Motherhood was really about. She could take part in the joys of learning about the unconditional love that comes between most Mothers and their children.

As her years of Motherhood unfolded, Mary Lou learned deeper lessons about life, love and fulfillment. As a wife, she gained a true awareness about fulfilling each vow of marriage until death darkened those marital promises. In her Motherhood, Mary Lou found new meaning to Pearl's decision about giving her away before birth.

Every time Mary Lou had another child, she was confronted with thoughts of "how could" and "why did" her own Mother give her away. And with every birth, I'm sure Mary Lou wrestled with deep emotions as she held her own babies immediately after giving birth and beginning the "bonding process."

One day when I asked my Mother what having a baby was really like, she responded by saying,

"It's like the worst and most painful bowel movement that you could ever have. But, when they give you your beautiful little baby, you quickly forget about all the pain because of the love that you have for your child."

That was one of the most visually descriptive statements that my Mother ever shared with me. She was expressing what most mothers' sentiments should be after childbirth.

Regardless of the physical pain, (in most cases) it should be only natural for a Mother to want bonding with her child in every sense of that human experience. Acceptance, affirmation, approval and unconditional love are the psychological arms that most parents embrace their children with from birth until death. For the most part and under normal circumstances, I don't think God ever intended for Mothers to give their children away. If God did intend that, why would He choose to bless those women with children in the first place? Only God can give life.

Every woman cannot have a child. Some will never choose to have any children or may not have the medical ability to even conceive one. At the end of the day, for the most part, those who have been graced by God to bring children into this world, should embrace their Motherhood by truly celebrating the awesome and miraculous gift of being a Mother.

My Mother found out how blessed she was to experience that kind of joy three times, when God gave her the gift of raising her own children. The blessings of having babies was a bridge toward deeper insights about her own birth mother, Pearl Battle. As a mother herself, now Mary Lou had an entirely different dimension to access, when it came to the actions surrounding her birth.

The most beautiful thing about this part of the scenario is that Mary Lou never rejected Pearl. Neither did Mary Lou teach her own 3 children to show any indifference, disrespect or rejection toward Pearl. My siblings and I were taught to unconditionally love *BOTH* Grandmothers, Pearl and Mary Louise.

Never, ever did any of us ever witness even one unkind word spoken from my Mother to either of her Mothers. Whenever we went to Cleveland, both Grandmothers were always visited. One was not placed above the other and both were esteemed as equally important by our Mother, Mary Lou. That is one of the main things that made me love and appreciate my Mother even more. She honored **both** of her Mothers with the finest respect that could have been given.

Although my siblings and I felt the awkwardness that sometimes stood between our Grandmother Pearl and our own Mother, we still were proud of our Mother for being the proverbial "bigger person" and also for taking the proverbial "higher road" as she honored the woman who promised to give her away before conception. Every time she honored Grandmother Pearl, Mary Lou was also showing everyone the forgiveness of God in spite of the deliberate and initial rejection from her own birth mother.

As I write this Chapter, now in 2017, I've experienced 4 years to the date since my Mother's death. Each day, week, month and year reveals new meanings to me concerning the journey of my Mother's life. As I miss her physical presence in my life, I can only now begin to imagine how deep of a pain that it must have been to have walked in the shoes that Pearl Battle gave to my Mother.

We, as our Mother's children, also witnessed the aftereffects of Pearl's prenatal choice to abandon our Mother. I remember those specific times in my childhood, when we went to visit Grandmother Pearl. She would open her apartment door with dramatics that Hollywood has yet to see.

Upon my mind's visual screen and my memory's untouched audio, I can vividly remember hearing Grandmother Pearl cry, while she so boldly stated,

"My child, my child, Mary Lou, you know that I did not mean to give you away."

This picture shows our Grandmother Pearl picking apples with her second oldest son and our Mother's older brother, Felix Battle. It's easy to see the strength of her personality in her stance and facial expression.

Then she would embrace our Mother and tell her that she loved her. During one particular visit, I also remember how Grandmother Pearl gave a short explanation as to how she had been having so many babies and Mary Louise didn't have any. She proceeded to say,

"Your Aunt Mary Lou wanted a child so bad and she saw me having one child right after another until she told me that one of my children could live with her. I was tired after I had Felix, so I told her she could have my next baby, if I had a girl."

I had never heard my Grandmother ever go into any detail about giving my Mother away. It seemed that she was feeling lots of remorse on that particular visit. Yet, it was truly humbling to see the strength of such an incredibly strong woman let go of all pride within those moments of explanation and contrition. There were no words given from our Mother. She just stood quietly and listened to Grandmother Pearl. When we left that day, I could still clearly remember Grandmother standing outside on her third floor balcony waving and saying, *"Bye Mary Lou!"*

She watched us until we walked out of her sight and around the corner to our car. A long part of the trip back home to Toledo was filled with contemplative silence. My heart was turned towards my Mother's heart. That was an extremely deep day for my Mother, her Mother and I.

It was quite emotional and awkward for me as a young child. I did not fully understand it then as I do now as a reflecting adult. I believe that behind all of my Grandmother Pearl's emotional outbursts there were true hidden sorrows and regrets for what she had done so many decades ago. Her regrets were deeply attached within the chambers of her mind. Like anchored weights, those undeniable regrets had not been lifted from my Grandmother's memories. She had not forgiven herself for giving her seventh child away and with that remorseful guilt she could not feel free from the residue of one poor decision.

Even after the decades since 1925, Pearl could not release the mental bondage of what her own calculated choice had cost not only her, but also her husband, Joel and her other eight children. The price of her decision had cost her far more than she had ever intended to pay.

On that particular day and in those revealing moments, my Grandmother seemed like she could no longer keep her innermost confession to herself. Grandmother Pearl wanted Mary Lou to know that she regrettably made a horrible decision as a Mother, wife and woman. If she never, ever again had the chance to communicate those sentiments to Mary Lou, Pearl made it known, without hesitation on that day. Yet, the depth of Mary Lou's silence seemed to give no consolation despite the intensity of my Grandmother's confessions.

Mary Lou's silence was often a way of not only being respectful, but also her way of escaping communicating about issues that were painfully deep. At times, our Mother's silence was like a frozen door of ice that could not be opened. That door barricaded others from the innermost thoughts within Mary Lou's soul. Only God knew what Mary Lou was thinking on that particular day. If I could have, I would have given my Mother permission to release every thought and emotion that she was feeling and thinking within that time and space.

Our Mother had never been emancipated from Pearl's decision of giving her away to Mary Louise. Although Mary Lou had not allowed Pearl's decision to dominate her from living a productive and self-fulfilling life, Mary Lou was as normal as any other individual who ever lived with the challenges, wonderment and questions of being given away from their birth family.

Years of maturing had not changed those factors and Pearl felt those truths in a mighty way, especially when in the presence of her seventh child. Pearl's maternal memories were void of unspeakable experiences that would never be known because of her choice to give Mary Lou away before conception. That was the sad and regrettable reality that Pearl's heart harbored.

That same reality was one of the factors that gave Mary Lou the determination to become the Mother that she was to her own three children. Mary Lou's Mindset propelled her far beyond the standards and levels of Pearl's choices as a mother.

King James Bible

Two are better than one; because they have a good reward for their labor. For if they fall, the one will lift up his fellow: but woe to him that is alone when he falleth; for he hath not another to help him up. Ecclesiastes 4:9

CHAPTER 4
Blessed Beyond Burdens

"For Better or Worse, In Sickness and in Health"

No one could ever argue the fact that Mary Lou had experienced her share of burdens long before she had ever met and married Hugh Washington. Neither could anyone deny the fact that her life had been filled with one challenge after the other. On one occasion when I was sharing some of my troubles with her, I remember her saying,

"Michelle, life is hard."

Who better could tell me that than one who had endured so many hardships? Having had the benefit of watching the resilience of Mary Louise in times of turbulence, gave Mary Lou the edge when trials came her way. Mary Louise had postured some of the best examples of mentoring.

One of the greatest trials of Mary Lou's marriage came on one March Morning in 1964. As Mary Lou stood looking out from their back bedroom window, she watched Hugh walking to the car to leave for work. As he got closer to the garage, he started struggling to walk. With immediate concern, Mary Lou went to Hugh who had fallen before the time that she reached his side. Once Hugh had been received at Mercy Hospital, the Doctors determined that he had suffered a severe stroke.

With all that Mary Lou had within her, she prayed for new direction from her dependable God. She did not allow this setback to overcome her for long. She had 3 dependent children.

Hubert was now 15 and away in Pottstown, Pennsylvania at *Pine Forge*, a Seventh-day Adventist Boarding Academy. Marla was turning 8 and in Grade 3 during the month that Hugh's stroke occurred. I was three years old and totally devastated by my Father's illness. Our entire family circle had been changed and totally rearranged because of the kind of hard working husband, father and provider that Hugh had been.

Hugh Washington was a man who believed in making sure his family was well taken care of at all times. His consistency to faithfully remain on the same job for 22 years was a clear indication about the mindset that he had about being a serious provider for his family. From sending money to help Mary Lou with her college tuition at Oakwood, on to later fulfilling his financial responsibilities as her husband and their children's father, Hugh never fell short taking care of the family that he so dearly loved. My Father was *"beyond happy"* to be the man that his family could depend on.

Pictured are Mary Lou and Hugh in Cleveland during their engagement, on the left side of the collage. The picture on the right is of them dressed for the Pastoral Installation Banquet of Pastor William Deshay at Bethel SDA Church in Toledo. This was shortly before Hugh would experience his paralyzing stroke.

This is a picture from our West Coast Summer Vacation. Hugh did almost all of the driving from Toledo to Arizona and then on to the Los Angeles, Perris and California areas where Mary Lou's sisters lived. This trip was the last family vacation that our Father gave us. Months later, he had a stroke.

As a husband, Hugh never really wanted Mary Lou to work outside of the home. He was not being chauvinistic in his thinking. Hugh just wanted to financially take care of his family by himself. My father did not mind working. He was a professional truck driver by day and definitely a loving and committed husband and father by night. On the weekends, Hugh was all about his wife, who he affectionately called "*Bunny*." He was also about spending plenty of quality time with his three children. In every way possible to him, Hugh shared his very best provisions.

This is a family portrait taken of Hubert, with his parents Mary Lou and Hugh around 1950. He was sleepy after a long day at church and Sabbath Dinner in Cleveland.

Photography Credits: Mr. Lucian Dixon

Every Friday, Hugh would faithfully bring his paycheck home, lay it on the table and say,

"Here Bunny."

Hugh was man enough to trust Mary Lou to handle the money that he earned. After all, she was the one who had earned the college degree in Business. Mary Lou was also the one who had shown Hugh just how skillful she was as an accountant. Mary Lou could take a dollar and make it holler, because she stretched it so hard. Hugh was extremely proud of the way that Mary Lou had helped him purchase not only his childhood home from his parents, but also an additional home when the family grew larger. He was more than satisfied with what he and his wife had accomplished as a team.

In this new hardship that Mary Lou was now facing, she had to dig deeper than ever before to find a new inner strength like never before. As a dedicated Mother, Mary Lou was resolutely focused on seeing her children through this difficult time. Not knowing exactly what all would be involved as she pressed forward, Mary Lou leaned upon the everlasting promises of a God that she had trusted in times past.

Mary Lou did not have time to waste in sorrow because she had to keep the mortgage, utilities, insurance for the car and the house, as well as tuition for Marla and Hubert all paid within their regular due dates. Now there were the additional costs of medical bills from Hugh's hospitalization and rehabilitation. Food had to be bought and clothes had to be provided for 3 children. Then there was the upkeep of 2 homes. One was their former home that was their rental property. The other was the house that they were now buying and living in. Money had to be available for any emergency or repair for either house. In addition, taxes had to be paid on those properties.

To make matters more complicated, *The George L. Freeman Lumber Company* who Hugh had worked for throughout the past 22 years, refused to give him his retirement even though he was only "*two weeks away*" from receiving it. They could have counted his vacation time as fulfillment of those 2 weeks. **Nevertheless, they remained immovable and refused to do so.**

For twenty-two years of dedicated and loyal service, my father received absolutely nothing but his final check. No severance package, no medical insurance or any other benefit that would have been due to him upon his retirement was given to him. His faithfulness of over two decades of service to his employer meant nothing.

Hugh David Washington had always been a dependable, respectable and favorable employee. He loved his work. His employers and also his customers highly regarded the stellar service that he consistently gave with a hearty smile.

In addition, Hugh's work ethic and work record had always been outstanding. Yet, he could not benefit from the stellar service that he had provided because the same employer that he had been faithful to, was unfaithful to him. Considering the fact that it was 1964 and that Hugh was "A Black Man in America", clearly made an impact upon his situation. If Hugh had been "a white employee" in the same situation, then the outcome would have probably been in his financial favor.

It's so amazing what "black skin" will exclude you from in this country that sings, *"My country 'tis of thee, sweet land of liberty"*. Even more amazing is the fact that within the same moments of singing the words, " *Oh say does that star spangled banner yet wave, o'er the land of the free and the home of the brave"*, some of the most outrageously unkind acts of bigotry are still taking place on American Soil, towards people of color.

What happened to Hugh Washington in that season and on that day, happened to his entire household. Each one of us were affected by one, ugly administrative decision of inhumanity, intolerance and cruelty. But it was my Mother who was impacted the most. She was the one who had to make *immediate decisions* that would determine the future for each one of us. Hugh had been the faithful provider. Now Mary Lou had to assume his role as "*the breadwinner.*"

This 1964 Easter Sabbath picture of Hubert, Marla and Michelle shows us standing behind our Rambler Station Wagon at our Clay Avenue Home. The Evergreen and Apple Trees are in the background. Also shown is our Father's Garage, "Man Cave" on the left side, far background. Mary Lou and Hugh were serious Sabbath keepers. My Mother did not tolerate lateness for church. We had to be ready with Sabbath Clothes in tact. On Friday evening we sang, "Don't Forget the Sabbath", (see link), https://rb.gy/np1rra while our Mother played the piano. No matter how late we had our musical Friday Night Family Song Fests, we were always on time for Sabbath School the very next morning.

Although the administrative actions of the George L. Freeman Company toward my Father were horrific, the *Mindset of Mary Lou* refueled and rebounded through reviewing who God had been in previous times of difficulty. When the concerned and inquisitive gossipers started making negative assumptions concerning Hugh's stroke and his family's point of need, *Mary Lou's Mindset* focused toward her God. When some family members, friends and neighbors questioned,

"Mary Lou, what are you going to do?"

Mary *Lou's Mindset* then claimed the promises of God to strengthen her faith and human weakness. Mary Lou also pointed her daily prayers of faith toward the God who she had trusted in times past. One of the hymns that she lived by was, **"Did You Think to Pray?"** Use the link to hear the song's message:

https://www.youtube.com/watch?v=2NSFmCduZGU

My Mother took the best of what she had learned from Pearl and Mary Louise and she used it towards her advantage in this time of turbulence. Every positive lesson that she had learned from both Mothers were now her greatest blessings beyond the burdens that at times seemed unstoppable.

Pearl was an extremely talented and self-taught woman. She had not had the privilege of attending a special school like Mary Louise. However, she had the special talents from God and the determination to accomplish whatever she attempted to do. Pearl played the harmonica, juice harp, and accordion. She made her own clothes and designed her own patterns to make them. She was one of the best cooks that I have ever known. Her sweet potato pie was so good that I have **NEVER** tasted any other one that tastes like it. Her recipe is still unmatched to this day. My Mother always said, *"Mama can make the best sweet potato pie and only use 2 or 3 sweet potatoes to make 4 or 5 pies."*

Our Grandmother Pearl was ahead of her time because if Hollywood had ever known about her, the entire Battle family would have been famous. While riding on a flight from Cleveland to Los Angeles, she took out her accordion and had the whole plane singing, *"Oh When the Saints Go Marching In."* The stewardess who wheeled her chair out to the gate to meet my Aunt Cassie said, *"Your Mother was such a delight to have on our flight. She kept the whole plane entertained."*

Pearl Catherine Battle

This picture was taken in December 1972 at Hubert's Wedding Reception. It shows Grandmother Pearl with 4 of her daughters and 2 of her sons. Seated in the front row left to right: Cassie, Hazel, (their Mother), Pearl, Daisy and then Mary Lou who is seated on the right end. Behind them standing, left to right, are two of Pearl's sons Felix and Henry. Photography Credits: Mr. Lucian Dixon

Nothing ever seemed to phase the courage of Pearl, if she decided that something was going to happen. One of the boldest yet funniest things I ever heard her say was about the *"hoodlums"*, as she called them, who lived in her troublesome and tough neighborhood. Upon one visit to her Cleveland, 75th and Lagrange Street Apartment, my Mother asked her,

"Mama, why don't you move away from here because every time you go to California to see Hazel, Cassie and Mattie, (3 of my Mother's older sisters), they break into your apartment. Aren't you worried about them breaking in on you while you are here?"

Without letting a second pass, Grandmother Pearl emphatically told my Mother,

"Child those hoodlums can break in here if they want to. I'll get my pistol and blow them all away!"

In that instance, I saw that the courage of my Grandmother was like that of Harriet Tubman. Although she was laughing and made all of us laugh, she was 100 percent serious. She went on further to explain how she had heard a noise at her back door one night. Rather than calling the police, she decided to get her pistol and then she said that she quietly eased back to the door from her bedroom. She said,

"Child, I could hear those hoodlums laughing and talking so I waited for them to put their hands on the door. When they started fumbling with the doorknob, I took my pistol, tapped on the door and said,

"You can break in here if you want to but I'll blow all your heads off if you do."

The funniest part of the story was when she said,

" After I said that, all I could hear was feet hurrying and scurrying down the back steps."

She was heartily laughing at her own story and as if she was reliving it again. My Mother also laughed with her as if they were having a duet of laughter between themselves. I could not laugh because I knew that my Grandmother Pearl meant every word of her pistol story and in that moment, my mind was imagining the outcome of the story if the hoodlums returned without luck the next time.

In so many ways Grandmother Pearl had passed her legacy of boldness unto Mary Lou. I will never forget the story that my mother shared about how one of her suits came up missing while she was a student at Oakwood. Mother told me the significance of how that particular suit was the very suit that she had personally designed and tailor made in her Central High School Home Economics Class. Her facial expressions and voice inflections embellished the story so well until I felt that I was watching the actual scene play out "live."

How could one of Mary Lou Battle's classmates even begin to think that they could pull that kind of skullduggery off with one of her belongings, is beyond me. That individual clearly did not know how quickly Mary Lou would defend herself when she was violated. The fact that it was a premeditated and intentional violation made it even worse.

For Mary Lou, there was only one solution for this issue of deliberate theft and she lost no time to handle her situation. Mary Lou simply went to the main corridor lobby of her dormitory and boldly announced with her most intimidating tone,

"My suit which I personally made is missing and someone in this dormitory knows where it is. It better be returned before this day is over or else I will find it for myself."

If that wasn't a "Pearl Battle" strategy, I don't know what else it could have been. Using the unashamed tactics of what her birth mother may have done in the exact same situation, is what Mary Lou unreservedly did with all of the spunk that she could find. With no nonsense, confrontational skills Mary Lou let the whole dormitory see that she could be as tough as Pearl when taking care of her own business.

With that kind of uncompromising approach, Mary Lou found her desired result. She ended the story by telling me,

"At the end of the day when I returned back from class, my stolen suit was hanging on the lobby doors. It was in the same condition as it had been before it was stolen."

That story has never left my memory. It still remains as evidence of how my Mother's personality could transform into an entirely unexpected avenue if it was provoked. The no nonsense side of Mary Lou was one that could not ever be forgotten by those who ignorantly challenged her defending spirit. To state things simply, "You did not want to mess with Mary Lou." She was truly about business and had no tolerance for foolishness, theft and intentional harm.

After that incident, Mary Lou never had any other occurrences of her personal items being stolen, while a student at Oakwood. I'm not at all surprised because she had set a bold boundary for thieves that was never again crossed. Mary Lou had demonstrated the same courage that Pearl had shown the neighborhood thieves who crept up her back apartment steps in Cleveland.

The Battle Family Group Photo, December 1972, at Hubert's Wedding Reception in Toledo, Ohio. (Toledo SDA School Gymnasium) Grandmother Pearl is on the front row, on the center seat, "surrounded by six of her nine adult children", seven of her grandchildren and several nieces and nephews. Photography Credit: Lucian Dixon

Pearl Battle was a woman of tremendous independence and strength. She is pictured above with 7 of her 9 adult children around 1964 at a family reunion held in Cleveland at her son, Felix's home. Felix was named after his Grandfather Felix, Pearl's father. Grandmother is seen standing with her children in their birth order. Left to right front row: Grandmother Pearl, Daisy, Hazel and Cassie. Back row left to right: Calvin, Felix, Mary Lou and Henry. The only two of Pearl's daughters who were not in attendance for this reunion was Mattie (Pearl's 4th child) and Catherine, (Pearl's 9th child) who was named after Pearl's Mother.

Pearl Battle was a woman of undeniably, incredible uniqueness. If her boldness could have been bottled and sold, our entire family would have been millionaires for life. I was always spell bound by the strength of her vibrant personality. It seemed as though there was nothing that could stop Grandmother Pearl if she decided that she was going to do something.

Genetically, she had come by her courage honestly. Her father, Felix Battle was the owner of 300 acres (a former plantation) of land in St. Joseph, Louisiana. Felix was also a father of 18 children.

Pearl had been born as a twin. *According to Cousin Turner Battle, III and the research he has done,* Pearl's twin sister died early or shortly after childbirth. That fact automatically placed Pearl as a surviving twin and her status truly matched her personality as "a survivor".

This is Mary Lou's maternal Grandfather and Pearl's Father, Felix Battle. Research regarding Great Grandfather Felix Battle is shared by courtesy and research of Dr. Turner Battle, III. Great Grandfather Felix was strictly about business. He had to have been because he and his wife Catherine were the parents of "18 children".(Some documentation records Grandfather Felix and Grandmother Catherine had 23 children.)

Carnton

Felix Battle was born in 1851 on a plantation in the Nolensville area of Williamson County. During the Civil War he lived for a time in a refugee camp on Granny White Pike in Nashville. When he was just thirteen years old, he enlisted as a musician in the 13th United States Colored Infantry. He participated in the fighting at Johnsonville as well as the Battle of Nashville. Battle was among the roughly 180,000 black men who served not only to attain their own freedom, but to save the Union. He mustered out with his unit on January 10, 1866. After the war he relocated to Tensas Parish, LA where he married Catherine Evans. Together they raised a large family. Battle was a successful farmer and sent his children to school in Nashville. In the early 1900s, he served on several grand juries of his local district court system. Felix Battle died in 1927 at the age of 76.

That is the information that The Carton History Museum in Franklin, Tennessee placed on Facebook regarding Felix Battle. He was definitely a real man of substance and valor. It is not hard to see where Pearl's courage came from. After reading that brief life sketch about Great Grandfather Felix, one can easily understand that Mary Lou's genetic pool was certainly filled with great determination and strength. Felix was the owner of a 300-acre former plantation in St. Joseph, Louisiana. He had 123 families working on the land that was called Lake Misery.

Standing by Great Grandfather Felix's side on that former plantation was a woman of great strength and tenacity. The fact that she was the mother of 18 children was enough to classify her as being strong.

Pictured next are 8 of Felix and Catherine's 18 children. Pearl Battle, Mary Lou's Mother, was one of those 18 children. Pearl is not in the next picture.

In this picture Mrs. Catherine Battle (wife of Felix Battle) is the first (right to left) seated in the rocking chair. Surrounding her are 8 of the 18 children that she birthed, mothered and raised with her husband Felix. Seated in the front middle is their son, Dr. Solomon Battle, Alumnus of Meharry Medical School. Seated next to him is his sister, Martha. Six of the Battle daughters standing on the back row, (left to right) are: Alva, Cassie, Catherine, Gertrude, Olivia and Mary Alma. Olivia was the oldest of the 18 and attended Oakwood as a student. The family was gathered to attend the funeral of Daniel Battle, Catherine and Felix's son who died at 40 years old of tuberculosis on February 27, 1926. Historical Information on Felix & Catherine Battle Family Credits: Dr. Turner Battle, III

Great Grandmother Catherine was introduced to the Seventh-day Adventist message through an African American man who worked with Edson White, (the son of Ellen G. White) on the Morning Star Boat. After selling a religious book to Catherine, she desired to receive lessons to learn more about the Bible. Catherine became a Seventh-day Adventist as a result of receiving Bible Studies from that colporteur who assisted Edson White.

The following link provides an audio presentation of Dr. Ron Graybill's lecture about Edson White's Ministry and Work in Mississippi on the Morning Star Boat. https://youtu.be/OwLf_iBERHQ?si=ylxPtXFhohbNdloB

Emma and James Edson White

The Mississippi River boat The Morning Star. *It featured a home for church workers, a chapel, and a printshop.*

Edson White was the son of Ellen G. White, who was one of the Oakwood University Founders. He is pictured above with his wife, Emma. Edson's ministry on the Morning Star Boat led many African Americans to Adventism in Mississippi and bordering cities. Pictured on the next page is the bell from the boat that was used during Edson's leadership within those southern areas. The Morning Star Bell has resided at the Oakwood University Archives for many years due to a cooperative agreement with Andrews Adventist University.

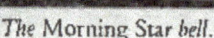

The Morning Star *bell*.

As the Battle Matriarch of her 18 children, Great Grandmother led her family to a new denominational faith. This discovery also led her oldest daughter, Olivia to be taught of the Lord at Oakwood. *Please see videos on page 257. Also see pages 279 and 280 to reference additional information about Oakwood University.)* The link below shares the information about the movie pertaining to Ellen White and Edson White's Ministry and vision for The Morning Star Missionary Story. https://rb.gy/87zh42 Edson White used his book, *The Gospel Primer* to finance his Morning Star Ministry and he also used it to teach those who were receiving lessons from this evangelistic and educational project.

Pvt. Felix Battle

1844-1927

Pvt. Felix Battle was born in October 1851 in Williamson County. It is believed that he was held in slavery by Charity Ann Horn Battle (daughter of Isaac Battle) and her husband Martin Clarke. The white Battle family took Felix back and forth between Louisiana and Tennessee when he was a small child.

He was the youngest Williamson County USCT soldier when he enlisted on April 6, 1864 in the 13th USCI. He was described as a 13-year-old laborer and was assigned to be a musician, probably a drummer boy. ; Dec. 17, 1864 sick in hospital in Nashville; He survived the War, including the Battle of Nashville, to muster out with his regiment on Jan. 10, 1866 in Nashville.

About a year later, Felix Battle appears to have enlisted in the 38th Infantry of the regular army as a so-called Buffalo Soldier. Enlisting with him was 1st Sgt. George Jordan, also from Williamson County. These were the first Black regiments created following the abolition of slavery in the U.S. He served one year and was discharged at Fort Bliss, El Paso, Texas on January 3, 1870.

About a year later, Felix Battle appears to have enlisted in the 38th Infantry of the regular army as a so-called Buffalo Soldier. Enlisting with him was 1st Sgt. George Jordan, also from Williamson County. These were the first Black regiments created following the abolition of slavery in the U.S. He served one year and was discharged at Fort Bliss, El Paso, Texas on January 3, 1870.

Battle later moved to Tensas Parish in northeast Louisiana where her married his wife Catherine Evans in 1873. The couple had 23 children and Felix Battle was a successful and well-respected member of the community. He served on several juries, could read and write and owned his own farm. Most of her children were sent back to Nashville to attend school here and some stayed in the area.

He died on September 20, 1927 at his home at "Lake Misery" in Tensas Parish. He was described as "honest, energetic and faithful to duty." in his obituary published in the local paper. He was survived by s

A memorial paver in his honor was sponsored by Tommy & Sue Justis.

This information above was taken from the website link listed below. Please visit the link. https://rb.gy/8fivxa

Also see this you tube video: https://youtu.be/OwAlru-8k_A

Felix Battle, one of the oldest colored citizens of Tensas parish, died at his home at "Lake Misery" on Friday morning, aged about 81 years. "Old Man Felix," as he was commonly known, was one of the best of his race, was honest, energetic and faithful to duty and always lived a clean and upright life. Born in slavery times he was owned by a prominent family of Tensas parish and was trained in right living, from which he never departed. His entire life was an object lesson to his race, for he knew how to work and save. He and his faithful wife lived together in peace and contentment for over fifty years and raised a large family of boys and girls, who have been a credit and comfort to them. All of his long life Felix enjoyed the respect and esteem of white and colored alike. He was a successful farmer and owned his own property. May he rest in peace!

Great Grandfather Felix's information above is also listed at the following website. https://www.slavestosoldiers.org/us-colored-troop-veterans/infantry-regiments/13th-us-colored-infantry The above clipping was probably listed as a newspaper obituary notice.

Aunt Cassie and Grandmother Pearl during one of her visits in California.

Pearl Battle was not shy of courage by any means. She knew how to handle herself and had no problem being courageous. While growing up, I had also witnessed that same courage of my Grandmother Pearl within my Mother whenever she confronted an issue of racism, injustice or any other incorrect matter. Although raised by Mary Louise, my Mother had been born with some of Pearl's genetic characteristics. That courage and boldness of Grandmother Pearl kicked into my Mother's spirit every time she had to stand her ground. Then having to transition into Hugh's role as the head of the household gave Mary Lou a constant, innate need to utilize those courageous skills that she had gained from Pearl.

Just like her birth Mother, Pearl, Mary Lou could also truly be a force to be reckoned with if you were the one against her and positioned as her opposition. Poised with the grace and dignity that she had learned from Mary Louise and born with the courage and spunk that she had received and observed from Pearl, Mary Lou could truly be someone that you did not want to mess with. Then, when she matched all of that, with her personal skills and educational training, one did not want to challenge her intelligence with foolishness.

Although there were burdens to bear at this time of Hugh's stroke and rehabilitation, there were still many blessings to share within Mary Lou's life. After a temporary time of receiving public assistance and before Hugh's social security disability benefits started, Mary Lou was able to once again utilize the skills that she had been taught while working on her degree at Oakwood College.

The Toledo Public Housing Authority hired Mary Lou to become a bookkeeper for their Ravine Park Village Site. While remaining on that job for 12 years, Mary Lou utilized all the professional business skills that Mr. Charles Galley, her favorite teacher from Oakwood, had taught her.

She was bonded by the financial and armored *"Brinks Company"*. Within the 12 years that she collected the rents for the Ravine Park Village Office and Birmingham Terrace Office, she was **NEVER** short for any of her deposits, not even by *"one penny."*

Her supervisor, Mr. La Rue, trusted Mary Lou beyond the shadow of any doubt. He trusted her so much that he basically left the office under her care while he was attending to other sites and while he was also heeding the many other supervisory roles that he had to fulfill. He was never worried about Mary Lou because he knew she was thoroughly competent and extremely trustworthy.

So what the *George L. Freeman Officials* had decided *against* Hugh and Mary Lou Washington, God turned around and brought good out of it for them and their children. Beyond the burdens were continued blessings. The tenants at Ravine Park Village treated Mary Lou like she was part of their own families.

At that time, Ravine Park was like a "melting pot" of cultures. There were Polish, Hungarian, Italian, German, Spanish, African American and Caucasian families all living within that community. The beauty of it all was how mostly all of the tenants appreciated, loved and respected our Mother, Mary Lou. Whenever I had to be dropped by her office after school, I was then learning from my favorite mentor, as I watched her fulfill her workplace duties with dignity, honor and grace.

It was a wonderful thing to see my Mother in such a role of trust while watching her serve a public housing community with well over 200 tenants. Everyone was treated with the utmost respect and professionalism. The beauty of my Mother's joy always left her customers feeling encouraged and well received.

On her busiest days, when it was around the first of the month, it was like watching a movie to see her count all of the rent money, balance her books and prepare the money for the walk-in safe that was in her office. Being her daughter did not ever allow me the privilege to go behind the service counter within her office. It was a known and unspoken fact that I *must* sit quietly on the waiting area chairs until she had completed her duties and was ready to turn the "office closed" sign around, on the door. That's what made my Mother the professional that she was. Even in the *"little things"*, she did not allow anything or anyone to keep her from exemplifying excellence at all times.

All those days of working within all those different homes while helping Mary Louise domestically serve all of those different families, had been preparation for

Mary Lou's role in public service. She had been well mentored by the woman who raised her, which was Mary Louise. She had also been well challenged by the woman who birthed her, which was Pearl.

Mary Lou is studying in Mr. Charles Galley's Business Class in 1947. Mary Lou is seated directly in front of her favorite Oakwood College Professor and Mentor. He is seen standing behind her viewing his class during instruction.

The knowledgeable blessings from being taught within Mr. Galley's accounting class, had taught her to be accountable for every penny under her watch. Mary Lou had the highest respect for her Oakwood Professor and Mentor, Mr. Charles Galley. She never forgot the instructional challenges Mr. Galley had given to his students to prepare them for their future careers. One of those unforgettable challenges Mary Lou easily remembered was when Mr. Galley gave her class an accounting problem of finding *"one penny"* to balance an account. She said that it took almost an entire night to find that penny and complete the assignment successfully.

Yet, it was those kinds of precise instructional directives that helped prepare Mary Lou for both of her government accounting positions in Rossford and Toledo, Ohio, years after her Oakwood Graduation. All of those life preparations which Mary Lou had experienced from Mary Louise, Pearl and Oakwood, were blessings that taught her to get beyond some of her most important challenges as a wife, mother and professional.

Even after graduating from Oakwood, Mary Lou kept her precious Oakwood Memories and friendships near to her heart. From time to time she shared some of her priceless experiences that had helped to shape her collegiate days. Whenever she reminisced about those Oakwood Years, Mary Lou painted a colorful, verbal picture that was easily received and understood. She never lost sight of how fortunate she had been to have been a part of "The Oakwood Experience", even if it was only for two years.

One of Mary Lou's precious Oakwood Memories came from an encounter that she had while walking across the campus one day. She shared it in this way,

*"When I attended Oakwood, everyone knew everybody who was on the campus. We were all like one family and known by our names. Our instructors and leaders took a special interest to guide us. I loved going to the "Old Mansion" to visit "Mother Cunningham". **(Please see pages 263 & 280 to see the picture of the Old Mansion and to read more information about Eugenia Cunningham)** She was a very kind lady. I also enjoyed going to Elder and Mrs. Peterson's house. I was friends with their daughters.*

I'll never forget the day when I was walking across the campus and President Peterson stopped me and said,

'Miss Battle, I need you to come to my office to dictate a letter.'

I don't remember where I was going or what I had to do at the time. All I remember is immediately stopping and going to the President's Office and taking the dictation. In those days, we highly regarded our leaders."

Almost a decade later, when our sister, Marla was born in 1956, Elder and Mrs. Peterson came to Toledo. Elder Peterson was coming to deliver the Sabbath Sermon for church. After the service, he inquired with Hugh about Mary Lou. When Elder Peterson found out that Mary Lou was still in the hospital after Marla's birth, Elder and Mrs. Peterson took time out to go and see Mary Lou at Riverside Hospital. It was those kinds of meaningful and intentional experiences of Oakwood Bonds that kept Mary Lou appreciative about being an *Oakwood Alumna.*

This photo of President Frank L. Peterson is on page 10 of the 1946 Oakwood Yearbook. (Find more information about Elder Peterson on pages 272 & 273 within the Additional Credits Section.)

PETERSON FAMILY

Oakwood College President's home, 1940.

Pictured above is President Peterson with his wife and family. While a student at Oakwood, Mary Lou visited the President's home on several occasions because of her friendships with Elder and Mrs. Peterson's daughters. Photo Credits: *Mrs. Minneola Dixon's Article, Loma Linda University, Adventist Heritage Volume 17, no 1, Spring 1996*

https://youtu.be/NCvZBtod8WQ?si=aEEy0zGQ9cj-5PW4

King James Bible

A man that hath friends must shew himself friendly: and there is a friend that sticketh closer than a brother. Proverbs 18:24

New Living Translation

There are "friends" who destroy each other, but a real friend sticks closer than a brother. Proverbs 18:24

CHAPTER 5 PART 1
Blessings Beyond Bondage

"Sojourning Through Crisis During the Civil Rights Era and Beyond"

If one had to pick which decade was the most challenging within the almost nine decades of Mary Lou's life, one may be incapable of choosing one over the other. At almost every turn and within almost every decade, Mary Lou had lived with the bondage of racism, rejection and discrimination. She had felt the cold sting of Ohio's Midwestern, subtle racial indifferences while growing up. Mary Lou had also felt Alabama's southern, blatant, slaps of segregation that had surrounded her while a student in the Huntsville community. Then after she married Hugh, Mary Lou found herself fighting causes on behalf of her children's justice, to make sure that their educational privileges were equally fair. When her heart was open to share those intolerable acts of bigotry, she did so with such an articulate manner which always painted a vivid picture.

Some of the stories could not leave her mind because they were like mental anchors holding their place in her historical heart. Mother had been born in 1925, one year earlier before Queen Elizabeth's birth. Yet as far apart as their worlds were in distance and royal lineage, their lives were even further apart in events. Although Mary Lou was not a royal heir, she had a rich, royal spirit about her life, in spite of many hardships. She could truly agree with the line in Langston Hughes' "Mother to Son" poem, which reads,

"Life for me ain't been no crystal stair".

Beyond all of the bondage that Mary Lou had lived through prior to her marriage, there was even more that had transpired within her circle of family ties after Hugh's stroke. Within the 1960's and 70's there seemed to be incidental events that were truly traumatic and "unforgettable". There was the tragic murder and death of her older brother, Calvin Battle that made the media news not only in Cleveland, but also in several other cities, because he had been shot and killed by one of his own son's associates.

That was just one of the deaths that left a mental anchor within my Mother's mind. She never really shared the sorrow that she felt about that loss. That was usually the way Mary Lou handled her deepest emotions. She held those emotions privately and almost as if they were buried treasure, because she was the only one who knew all about them.

Mary Lou with six of her eight siblings and her birth Mother, Pearl in Cleveland. This photo was taken in 1964 at a Battle Family Reunion at Mary Lou's brother's (Felix) home.

From left to right (front row) Grandmother Pearl, Daisy,Hazel,Cassie

From left to right (back row) Calvin, Felix, Mary Lou and Henry

(Two of Mary Lou's sisters that were not able to attend were Mattie of Los Angeles, California and also Catherine of Cincinnati, Ohio.)

When the call came to our house about Uncle Calvin's murder, the news was so very heart wrenching, unbelievable and so unexplainable.

"Why? Why? Why?"

That was the unanswerable question for this horrendous crime.

Uncle Calvin was the perfect blend between both of his parents, Joel and Pearl. He had a vibrant personality that was contagious to most everyone that he met. Being easy on the eyes did not hurt him at all, as far as the ladies were concerned. He definitely had a special swag and confidence that was solid as stone.

Calvin is standing behind his Mother, Pearl. It is not hard to see that Calvin Battle was a handsome man. He was as bold and as comical as Pearl. Uncle Calvin held nothing back. Grandmother Pearl quietly listened when he gave her an ultimatum about what she needed to do concerning her wellbeing. Our Uncle Calvin took nothing off anyone. He was absolutely, 100 percent a real man who loved and looked out for family. In the last photo Uncle Calvin is standing alone.

Uncle Calvin had a way about himself that could charm a spitting cobra. He had a very keen and deep mind, like Grandfather Joel. Yet he could humor you as finely as Grandmother Pearl could, because he knew how to get your attention to make you laugh. On some of his trips to Detroit, he would stop by our home in Toledo and "check on his sister", as he would proudly announce. I loved that about him and so did our Mother. He always brought the gift of laughter with him and we needed some joy to take our minds away from our Father's illness.

Uncle Calvin was hard not to love, if you appreciate people "being real", because Calvin Battle was truly his own man and a real man in every sense of the word. There was nothing fake or phony about him and he had no problem calling things out for what they truly were.

Although Mary Lou did not always agree with her brother's choices, she loved him and respected the fact that he was never a pretender. His death was a very difficult time. For the first time, Mary Lou, along with her brothers and sisters learned about the shocking grief of losing a sibling so suddenly.

There was also the death of Mary Lou's nephew Larry Battle, who was the son of Mother's brother, Felix Battle. Larry was tragically shot and killed. His death so sadly occurred after returning back home to Cleveland with a medal of honor. He had received *The Purple Heart*, from serving in Vietnam. That was one of the saddest family funerals that I have ever attended.

This picture is at a birthday party in Cleveland. Larry is standing second in the back row (right to left) next to Hubert. Marla is in the front row. She is the second girl standing left to right with the bows in her hair. It was Daisy's, Larry's little sister's birthday. Daisy is the tallest girl standing in the second row next to Hubert.

Larry was one of the kindest people on the face of the planet. He was genuinely warm and pleasant in spirit. I don't ever remember anyone speaking about him being mean spirited. How could they, when Larry made everyone feel so comfortably affirmed? Love was a huge part of Larry's character.

Larry was the first of Mary Lou's nieces or nephews to die. Because of the close bond between Felix and Mary Lou, Larry's death was almost like losing one of her own children. It was tough for the entire Battle family because Larry was so well loved. Cousins, uncles, and aunts included, were all so very, deeply grieved to lose such a young family member that had so much life left to live and also so much love to give.

I still remember waking up from hearing the awful grief that came out of the phone from the voice of Aunt Eleanor, Uncle Felix's wife. Her grief sounded as if she would never recover from the loss of her son. When their call came on that early morning hour, it was like a bomb had gone off. This was another time when Mary Lou silently kept the depth of her feelings inside. Between the two deaths of Larry and then Uncle Calvin, for a while, I really did not want to hear my Mother say that we were going to Cleveland. Both of their deaths left a deep void in the family that could never be explained or replaced. When the bondage of death is not dealt with through the proper stages of grieving, then healing is delayed, while sorrow subtly lingers.

In addition to the murders of her brother and nephew, no one will ever truly know how Mary Lou emotionally handled her feelings about Hugh's stroke. For a huge part, it seemed like she never gave herself the chance to deal with all that she was feeling, because she was so involved in making sure the needs of her children, as well as her husband were met.

Thank God for those dear, true friends who stood by her side to encourage and emotionally support her at the time of Hugh's unexpected stroke. Though Mary Lou had no family members in Toledo, she had friends that were so close to her that they were just like family. Elder Frank Ashford and his wife Benetta as well as First Elder Charles Wilson were spiritual leaders at Bethel SDA Church. They were also close friends and supportive of Hugh and Mary Lou.

From left to right at the Bethel Church dedication are: L-R. Ernest Francis, Frank Ashford, Charles A. Wilson, William L. Cheatham (President of Allegheny Conference) James W.Thomas, (Bethel Pastor), Paul Cantrell and Burrell Scott. (Although an Oberlin resident, Burrell Scott and his wife Bonnie were just like extended siblings to Mary Lou and Hugh.) Our family spent many happy times with the Scott Family in Oberlin.

Essie Darnell was just like a sister to Mary Lou. They had such an especially close friendship until sometimes it almost seemed that they both had come out of the same womb. Both of them had July birthdays and both of them had a mind of their own. They both were not ashamed or afraid to speak their opinions to anyone regardless of a person's race, gender or social status.

Essie and Mary Lou were some strong minded black women. They did not compromise on a standard and they held firm to whatever they believed. It was a blessing that Mary Lou had such a dependable friend like "Aunt Essie", especially when she really needed some sisterly support that was right in town.

This is a picture of Essie Darnell (on the left side) of Mary Lou. They were at Hubert's wedding reception at the Independence Road SDA School Gym in Toledo. It was December of 1972. Photography Credits: Mr. Lucian Dixon

When Hugh had his stroke and Mary Lou was reluctant about visiting him each day at Mercy Hospital, because she did not want to see her husband in that condition, it was Essie that said,

"Mary Lou, you have to go."

It was also Essie and her devoted husband, Louis Darnell that never changed their acceptance of my Father throughout *all* the years of his illness. They never looked down on Daddy. Neither did they treat him as though he was pitiful like some individuals did. "Aunt Essie" and "Uncle Louis" were "true blue", "good as gold" friends until the very end of Hugh's life. They were part of the blessings that helped Mary Lou get through the bondage.

Photos from Essie & Karen Darnell's Personal Photos

Seated in the first picture above are Mr. & Mrs. Louis and Essie Darnell who were both born and raised in Mississippi. The middle picture is a 2020 photo of my awesome Godmother, Aunt Essie. She rode the bus from Toledo, Ohio to Louisville, Kentucky on August 20, 2013 with the intent to see her dear friend, Mary Lou. Knowing that Mary Lou was nearing her last days, Essie came ready to give to Mary Lou some of her signature cornbread dressing and sweet potato pies that she had packed in her carry-on bag.

As she was en route on the Greyhound Bus, Mary Lou passed before Aunt Essie's bus arrived in Louisville. Faithful to Mary Lou to the very end, Aunt Essie was the one who went with me and Eddie Green Sr. to the funeral home on the day of Mary Lou's death.

Karen "Louise" Darnell and David Darnell, Sr. are standing in the third photo.

Essie gave her only daughter, Karen, the middle name "Louise" in honor of her husband Louis and her dear friend, Mary Louise. Louis and Mary Lou were the two individuals who adamantly encouraged Essie during her fifth pregnancy. They both faithfully told Essie that she would have "a girl" throughout her last pregnancy.

Prior to that, she had given birth to "4 sons" and Essie did not believe that she was going to have her greatly desired daughter. On a sunny April Sabbath afternoon, Essie called Mary Lou to tell her that her newborn baby was "a girl". Of course that was one of the happiest days of Essie's and Mary Lou's friendship.

With the greatest and most joyous pride, Mary Lou was quick to remind Aunt Essie, "I told you that you were going to have a girl, Essie", on the very day of Karen's birth, while at Riverside Hospital. Pictured below is Essie and her 4 sons as boys.

MR. FLUTE RICE
Principal

Mr. Flute Rice was another faithful friend in Toledo that maintained deep sincerity to Hugh and Mary Lou during Hugh's illness. Although extremely involved in a myriad of career responsibilities within his administrative roles for The Toledo Board of Education and First Black Principal at Scott High School. "Uncle Flute" as my siblings and I called him, was always willing to encourage, support and listen to Hugh and Mary Lou.

Flute Rice was the individual who strategically recommended and guided Hubert into his very first teaching position and first job after graduating from Oakwood College in 1970.

For many years, Hugh and Flute Rice, along with George Harris Sr. and James Hill Sr. sang in a well-known Toledo Quartet named, "The Evangeliers". The quartet annually sang throughout the Toledo area raising Ingathering Funds during the Christmas Holiday Seasons. Always reaching and often surpassing their Ingathering Goal, the Evangeliers were well welcomed within the Toledo Community. Flute's tenor voice was one of an unforgettable and melodic cadence. His friendship to Hugh was earnest and true.

(Photos from Scott High School Toledo, Ohio) See page 274 for additional information.

This photo is a representation of the quartet, "The Evangeliers" singing at a Sabbath Church Service. (Bethel S.D.A. Church in Toledo). The only two original members seen in the photo are far left, James Hill and far right, George Harris. In the middle (next to James Hill) is James Banks who filled in for Flute Rice. Hubert Washington, sang on behalf of his father's baritone voice. James Hill and George Harris were also loyal friends to Hugh. (December 1974) Credit: Hubert Washington Photos

Dr. Nell Anthony was also another loyal friend who was also happy to show her faithful and loving friendship to Mary Lou and Hugh. "Aunt Nell" (my other Godmother) was one of those friends that was just like the Biblical description which refers to "a friend that sticks closer than a brother". She was Flute Rice's sister and also a stellar educator, administrator and mentor. Her years of service in the Education Department at Alabama A&M University were years of excellence and "first class leadership".

Dr. Nell Anthony also was abundantly liberal with her guidance, suggestions and professional critiques to Oakwood University's Education Department whenever they were facing any national or state accreditations. She worked unselfishly to share her expertise with any of Oakwood's Professors or Administrators who reached out for her assistance. She was truly a loving lady with impeccable standards of Christianity.

The third photo shows Leona Meredith, Nell Rice and Mary Lou at the wedding shower Mary Lou organized for Nell, prior to Nell's wedding to Professor Harold Anthony.

Professor Anthony is pictured on the right side of the photos on the preceding page.

Mr. Harold L. Anthony directed the Oakwood College Choir as seen in the 70th. Anniversary Album of the College. Hubert was fortunate enough to have been under Professor Anthony's musical leadership at Pine Forge Academy also. Mr. Anthony was a fine musician, composer and director. He composed the Pine Forge School Song and arranged the music for the Oakwood School Song. His service was always stellar.

Professor Anthony is standing on the front row, far right, on the album cover.

The complete 1966 album is in the following link.

https://youtu.be/RFxfshoBpjs

Pine Forge School Song in link:

https://youtu.be/wzn4D90dKUk?si=9w615SE57FF-Bh-H

Oakwood School Song in link:

https://youtu.be/xoeDByELg8w?si=iWw3M8d2ixfGSGO7

Mr. Anthony's contributions to the Pine Forge, Oakwood and Huntsville communities were of excellence and also unforgettable wherever his choir toured nationally. His standards were consistently firm, fair and exceptionally high for his entire choir.

Pictured in the photo on page 115 is Nell Anthony and her sister, Gertrude. Both of them were marvelous friends to Mary Lou and Hugh. Aunt Gertrude was also an educator and she was an outstanding Reading Specialist for the Toledo Public Schools. Like her brother, Flute, she had a stellar reputation for being dedicated to her students. Gertrude was known for her "no nonsense" and professional mindset within and without the classroom. Mary Lou and Gertrude spent many, many hours on the phone talking, laughing and sharing their weekly experiences. Aunt Gertrude was truly a straight shooter who did not hesitate to voice her opinions. Her honesty was priceless and very much needed especially at times when there were critical issues to be decided.

She was a woman who had an incredible mind and impeccable taste. The last photo shows the entire Rice Family. Their history in Huntsville, Alabama is monumentally unforgettable and spans many decades. As a large, talented and influential family, they have made outstanding milestones within not only the Huntsville but also the Toledo communities. Please go to the following link to hear the oral interview with Flute Rice to learn more about the Rice Family and their history.

See additional information in the Credits Section of the back of the book. (page 274)

Photo Credit: Photo Copies from Dr. Nell (Rice) Anthony's Album

Then there were other friends that were also great blessings to Mary Lou in Toledo. Mary Hawkins was one of the very, very few people who could provide child care for Mary Lou's children. "Sister Hawkins" who later became Mary Williams after marriage, was the one that Mary Lou trusted with her children beyond any doubt.

For Mary Lou to trust *anyone* with her children, was an extremely high compliment because she was so selectively careful about the influence and protection of their wellbeing. This kind of protective wisdom had been mentored by Mary Louise's example so many years ago when she refused to let Ethel Waters take Mary Lou and raise her. Our Mother followed closely in the footsteps of the woman that she loved and admired.

Bertha Major, Essie Darnell, Jessie Talley, Mary Lou Battle-Washington and Sharon Hawkins are standing left to right in the above photo taken in Toledo.

I always enjoyed visiting the Major, Darnell and Talley Homes.

Jessie Talley, who ironically was the daughter of Mary Hawkins, was also another friend that Mary Lou knew she could trust with her children. "Sister Talley" was one of two or three people whose home my Mother allowed me to spend the night within the entire city of Toledo. As a child, I didn't fully know why my Mother was so selective. At that time, she seemed too strict.

After becoming a teacher and dealing with hundreds of families, I am so truly grateful for the faithful wisdom and protective choices of my Mom. My adulthood has taught me how one can never be too careful when allowing children into the homes of other individuals.

Beyond any doubt, now I know that our Mother's choices were those to make absolutely sure that Hubert, Marla and I were always safe. She was always looking out for our very best interests.

When I think about all the real people who made themselves available to lend their helping hands, prayers of persistence, words of wisdom and strong support to uplift my parents at the time of my Father's illness, it always makes me feel proud to know that I was born and raised in Toledo. Though the 60's and 70s were historically filled with lots of civil rights activism to release the bondage of the times, there were also great blessings unfolding for black people across the nation.

Mary Lou was a part of the activism within the educational arena of her church. She and Hugh had made bold strides to integrate the Caucasian Seventh-day Adventist Church School, then located on Auburn Avenue and called Goff Jr. Academy. With very few *exceptions,* one which was my Father's brother, Elbert, in 1954, Hubert was the only black child to be accepted through their school doors at the time. One would think that a church would be more liberal with its' standards of tolerance. That, however, was not the case at the time. Even now as I am writing this in 2017, although racial inclusion has occurred, the Seventh-day Adventist Church is still dealing with issues of racial indifference and division within some of their predominantly racially segregated congregations, schools and churches.

Although there are higher levels of integration within this denomination, there is still much more room for improvement when it comes to sincerity concerning tolerance as it relates to racial diversity and love for all people of color. Even now there are still color issues within this denomination that question the insincerity of true tolerance and diversity. If this is not the case, why does one still find white conferences and regional conferences within most divisions of the Adventist Church? The same reason that you find it in other denominations that have maintained the same racial divisions within their organizational structure. We hear people singing "We Shall Overcome" while we see them living "A Better Day After While" and remaining divided.

When Mary Lou decided that she would give her children the Christian Education that she never had, she had to first confront the mental bondage that

Hugh was carrying. Hugh Washington had received a public school education within the Toledo Public Schools. He felt that the same system which he had attended was good enough for his children.

Mary Lou would not agree under *any* circumstances. She relentlessly stood her ground and let Hugh know that her children would not attend 8 different schools within 12 different years before graduating from High School, like she had done.

Once Mary Lou had broken through the barrier of changing Hugh's position about Christian Education for their children, they both faced the smugness of the Goff Jr. Academy School Board. Having the second black child to attend this private Christian school was more than a hurdle in 1954. Being in a historical "free state" as Ohio was considered to be in the slavery era, did not mean that all hearts and minds were ready for change even though the Civil Rights Movement was developing with a momentum of its own.

When Mary Lou and Hugh sat before the Goff Jr. Academy School Board, they were boldly told, *"You can bring your son to our school, but you will have to buy a desk for him and also his school books."*

Hugh Washington firmly responded by saying,

"I don't think that it is fair that I should have to buy a desk and books for my son when I pay tithe to the same denomination that you pay tithe to. However, I will pay for my son's books and I will buy a desk for him. But when the school year is over, I will be bringing those books and his desk to my home where they will be stored for the summer."

After that brief reply from Hugh, one of the board members quickly replied, "Oh that will not be necessary. You don't have to buy a desk or books for your son."

Thus the second color barrier was broken at the Goff Jr. Academy, because of Mary Lou's Mindset upon her husband and her persistence to stand firm against Hugh's bondage about *paying* for Christian Education.

Her mindset influenced Hugh's mindset to make a move for a much needed change within the educational realm of the Seventh-day Adventist Church in Ohio. The irony of it all was that almost 20 years later, Hubert would also become the very first African American Teacher at that same school that later moved to Independence Road and is now operating on the Sylvania Avenue site. Mary Lou did not allow the bondage of others, *even her own husband's bondage,* to block her blessing for her son. Because of *Mary Lou's Mindset,* blessings came beyond the bondage.

mary Lou - Hugh

As a husband and a father, Hugh did not hesitate to let anyone know his intentions. *Hugh Washington was a warrior for his family. He wanted to give them his very best. In this photo, Mary Lou and Hugh are seen outside of their 1837 Homer Residence which they purchased from Hugh's Parents, David and Iscolar Washington.*

International Version

Share with the Lord's people who are in need. Practice hospitality.
Romans 12:13

King James Bible

Can two walk together, except they be agreed? Amos 3:3

CHAPTER 5 PART 2
Blessings Beyond Bondage

Before Mary Lou and Hugh could be on one accord about the issues of where their children would attend school, they had deep discussions about what they believed in as well as what was important to both of them. My parents had moments when their disagreements were like two ships passing in the night with different destinations. My Mother called it, *"agreeing to disagree"*. She was not going to change upon a position that she felt was right.

When they did not have a "meeting of the minds", silence was the standard for Mary Lou. Retreating to nature was the standard of choice for Hugh because he loved being outdoors. Hugh would also often head to the garage that was directly in the back of the house. There he would take time to dwell in his personal space which in today's world is known as *"a man cave"*. That was his time to take a step back and think.

Hugh and Mary Lou were never shy about voicing their opinions to each other. Neither did they back away from letting their voices be heard in social arenas where public opinions may not always be in sync with what they believed. Regardless of their personal views on issues, they usually found a way to come together when a decision had to be finalized. Sometimes it meant that one of them had to give way to the other because neither one of them were cowards.

Both my parents had a mindset *that was as steep as a mountain.* Had it not been for the loyal relationship that they had with God, their marriage may not have survived the challenges that they had to face as husband and wife. I say this because Hugh and Mary Lou both had bondage within their own individual lives long before they had ever met one another. Both of their lives had been complex in different ways.

In my estimation, it was my Father who usually gave way to my Mother. But Mary Lou also had moments of surrender when she chose to give in so that Hugh could have his way. One of those moments was when Mary Lou wanted to purchase their second home closer to the school where Hubert and Marla were attending. Each day Marla and Hubert had to catch 3 buses to reach the church school which was 20 miles away. Once they got off of their last bus, they had to walk almost 1 mile before they got to school, even on the snowiest and rainiest of days. This was their regular routine whenever they didn't get a ride to school. This was one of the reasons Mary Lou wanted to live closer to their school or live within the school neighborhood.

After all was decided, the home which was purchased was just two streets away from the first home which they had bought from Hugh's parents. Mary Lou knew that Hugh wanted to remain in his childhood neighborhood so she made the sacrifice for her husband. As strong willed as Mary Lou was, she was also in favor of *"keeping the peace"* within her home whenever she could.

After all, she had seen enough conflict between Pearl and Joel as well as Mary Louise and Wright while growing up. That was not the kind of emotional environment that Mary Lou desired for Hubert, Marla and Michelle.

If giving in to Hugh's choices every now and then meant happiness for her household, then she could furnish that happiness by yielding to *some* of her husband's decisions. Now please don't make any mistake about Mary Lou's yielding. She never compromised on any of her standards.

In those very special times when Mary Lou did choose to yield to Hugh's decisions, she did so with the mindset of upholding all the principles that had always been grounded within the depths of her heart. That's what made *Mary Lou's Mindset* so truly genuine.

Early on in their marriage, Mary Lou demonstrated her love to not only Hugh but also to his parents. She exemplified a living testimony not only to Hugh's family, but also to her family as well as all of the neighborhood and church families, concerning the quality of woman that she chose to be.

Hugh's Mother, Iscolar Washington was a sickly woman. Iscolar had been a stroke patient and her doctor had informed her and her husband David that they should move to a warmer climate. In order to do that, they had to sell their home so that they could purchase a new one.

Hugh and Mary Lou were the ones who purchased Hugh's childhood home so that his parents could buy a house outside of Phoenix where they had moved. This was not something that a new bride may have wanted to do. For Mary Lou, it was a choice about blessing her new family who had struggled with the bondage of not only Iscolar's sickness but also with the death of Hugh's sister and younger brother.

In that one decision, my Mother gained the lifetime respect of my Grandfather. Many decades later when our Grandfather David shared this story, he expressed his heartfelt respect and admiration for Mary Lou who he called *"daughter"*. He always affectionately called our Mother, "daughter" without any hesitation. It was his way of letting her know that he respected her just like she was his very own blood daughter.

Our Grandfather David also respected the fact that Mary Lou insisted upon *faithful* returning of church tithes and offerings within his son's home. Hugh was buying *five dollar neckties* when he married Mary Lou in 1947. *(The value of a 1947, $5.00 necktie in our 2024 economy would now value and cost $70.44.)* Prior to their marriage, Hugh had been inconsistently returning his tithes and offerings. When Mary Lou learned about this, she immediately informed Hugh on *"day one"* of their marriage that *"faithful tithes and offerings"* would be returned from their household. Mary Lou **never** changed her stance about this biblical standard. (*Malachi 3:10*) She wanted the blessings that God promised upon their home.

This is a picture of Hugh's Father and my Grandfather, David Washington at my 1982 Oakwood College Graduation. Grandfather David highly respected Mary Lou and affectionately called her "Daughter". Grandpa was a healthy "90 years old" and still legally driving (with a valid California License) at the time of this photo. (June 1982)

"Gramps" as I sometimes called him, was proud to always share how his son, Hugh and daughter- in- law, Mary Lou bought their home without ever being late on *any* of the payments.

Mary Lou's father- in- law, David Washington, had a stellar reputation within the Toledo Adventist Community. He had been a colporteur for the Ohio Conference during the Great Depression. This home that Mary Lou and Hugh were purchasing had also been the very home of hospitality where Dr. E.E. Cleveland had lived for several months while learning the colporteur work. This is documented in Dr. Jacob Justiss' book, *Angels in Ebony. (See page 270 to confirm and see additional information)* Brief remarks are also within the televised and personal interview that Elder Cleveland shared from the Oakwood University Church, *(See 3 ABN interview to confirm. At point 20:50 on the link, Elder Cleveland tells about "moving in with a colporteur", Elder David Washington*)

https://youtu.be/vxlgiYBcsCI

After graduating from Oakwood with the intention of receiving a ministerial assignment, Elder Earl Edward Cleveland was not immediately given a pastoral assignment. During that pivotal time of Elder Cleveland's life, he was uncertain of his future.

Feeling somewhat discouraged by the fact that he was without an initial ministerial assignment while at the same time feeling ready to marry his sweetheart, Celia Abney, was a time of difficult sojourning for him. This time period was a definite *challenging crossroad* for Elder Cleveland.

However, he found a spiritual haven within the *1837 Homer Avenue* residence of "the old colporteur". (as he referred to David Washington in the 3ABN interview) It was at that humble, Toledo Home of David Washington that Earl not only found a deeper understanding of practicing faith and prayer, but it was also where he first found the hymn, *"Lord in the Morning"*, (https://youtu.be/n5zzdz85Vb0?si=f95fXNmzMSoHmi4), as a daily anchor and morning family worship hymn. This was because the Washington Family faithfully sang it every morning during their family worship period. During one of Mary Lou's visits with Mrs. Celia Cleveland, it was Mrs. Cleveland who confirmed that Earl had adopted that exact same hymn within their own home for family worship. She said that they had sung it for their family worship throughout the many years of their marriage.

Within that time frame of mentoring Earl in Toledo, God allowed David Washington to have a dream which he shared concerning Earl's life. The very next morning after having the dream, Grandfather David shared the dream with Elder Cleveland in the following words,

"Earl, God gave me a dream about you last night. In the dream I saw where you were baptizing hundreds of people. Do not worry about getting a job. God is going to use you."

It was shortly after God gave this dream to David Washington, that Earl Cleveland received his very first pastoral assignment to serve as a minister in North Carolina. There he began the beginning of a phenomenal career that spanned over 70 years of **worldwide evangelism** for the Seventh-day Adventist Church. The future revelation and fulfillment of that dream greatly surpassed both the imaginations of "the old colporteur" and the unemployed ministerial Oakwood Graduate in the decades following those humble summer days in Toledo.

Yet, Earl never forgot what he had gained spiritually from his Toledo Mentor. In later years, whenever he came in contact with David Washington, Elder Cleveland was not shy to acknowledge and refer to that spiritual patriarch as "Dad Washington". Even in July of 2003, when his wife of over 60 years had just passed away in May of 2003, Dr. Cleveland unreservedly came to Mary Lou's daughter, Marla's funeral to give remarks. In the picture below, he is seen sitting on the platform at the Oakwood University Church. **See page 262 for additional info. About E.E. Cleveland.**

This first picture shows Dr. Earl Edward Cleveland in 2003 attending Marla's Funeral. The second picture shows Evangelist Cleveland preaching at a crusade. The last photo is of Dr. Cleveland and his lovely wife, Mrs. Celia (Abney) Cleveland.

https://www.youtube.com/watch?v=3FIX18zf5c0

Mary Lou's desire to support Hugh's wishes to purchase his childhood Toledo home at 1837 Homer Avenue was her way of showing Hugh that she could yield to his goals even though her own desires were not of the same choosing. She sacrificed her dreams for a ranch style, brick home to accommodate the choice that her husband wanted to buy. That decision demonstrated the unselfish heart that Mary Lou so naturally and lovingly had within.

Whenever my parents didn't see eye to eye about a matter, I always thought about the things that they had done in one accord. To me, their history was greater than any earthly challenge or disagreement that they could ever have. I never ever wondered if my parents would divorce as some children do when their parents disagree. Regardless of the dispute, I always felt that their love and respect for each other outweighed their differences. It was clear, even within the avenues of my young mind, that my parents were committed to each other.

This Thanksgiving Family picture was taken at the home of Virgil and Ernestine Humphreys in Belleville, Michigan. Ernestine was Mary Lou's cousin.

As I watched my Mother fulfill her vows of faithfulness during my father's illness, I witnessed two of the greatest aspects of her mindset, "*consistent morality and faithful loyalty.*" Mary Lou did not compromise her commitment to Hugh. Not even "one" time. Throughout my childhood, I watched her faithfully fulfill the promise of her vows,

"For better or for worse, for richer or for poorer, in sickness and in death, 'til in death we do part."

Although Mary Lou had some pretty eager admirers, even within the close proximity of our neighborhood, our Mother ignored their adulterous hints. She would not be swayed into their temptations of being unfaithful to her husband Hugh.

The virtues that she had been taught long ago by Mary Louise held firm within her heart. The foundational anchor of her character would not be moved. This was truly a noble part of our Mother's mindset.

This collage shows the loving loyalty that Mary Lou had for Hugh. Regardless of the season, as Hugh's health declined, Mary Lou still stayed by his side as she had done when he was younger and healthier.

Hugh was disabled for 11 years after having his stroke. Given the exact same circumstances, some women would have immediately sent him to a nursing home or they might have sent him to rehabilitate with his birth family in order to walk away from the responsibilities that are involved in providing the necessary care for a sick spouse. However, that was not an option for Mary Lou Battle. She was committed to her vows, "for better or worse, in sickness and health."

With not one, not two, but three dependent children, Mary Lou set her mind upon the blessings rather than the bondage. She did what needed to be done, *come rain or come shine.*

Throughout this 11-year period of Hugh's health decline, Mary Lou's Mindset would not weaken to compromise any of her standards as a wife, as a mother and most of all as a Christian who loved the Lord.

Hugh and Mary Lou are pictured cutting their wedding cake in June of 1947. The wedding was held in Cleveland at Mary Lou's childhood church.

I could never, ever write this story and fully give my Mother the accolades that she truly deserves to be remembered by, because I cannot fully find the words to express how monumentally marvelous my Mother's Mindset was especially during the turbulent times of trial and trouble. Mary Lou did not run when faced with adversity and her faith did not flinch when the future seemed uncertain. That's what I've missed the most about her being in my life, even though over seven years (*now 11 years at the current 2024 editing stage of this manuscript*) have passed since her death.

***This Christmas Family Portrait was photographed in 1966 of our family.
Photo Credits: Mr. Lucian Dixon***

Can you even begin to imagine what it was like to witness a 38-year-old woman pick up the shattered pieces for her family after her husband's debilitating stroke?

Can you comprehend the mental highs and lows that may have found their place within the emotional mountains and valleys of Mary Lou's Mind?

Keep in mind the journey that Mary Lou had already taken prior to aligning herself in marriage with Hugh. *There is no earthly imagination that can begin to paint the complex canvas of Mary Lou's Mindset.*

The fact that she chose to maintain a sense of consistency to all that was required of her as a daughter, niece, sister, cousin, wife, daughter in law, sister in law, mother, aunt, mother in law, nana, friend, neighbor, church member and also an employee, says so much about the woman of worth that Mary Lou Battle-Washington was within her core spirit. It is even more amazing that our Mother could choose to take her experiences of bondage and still strive to make those experiences blessings through choosing to activate her dependence, faith and obedience toward God.

Last, but not least, of being amazing, is the ultimate fact, that Mary Lou chose to consistently take the "dirty deeds" of those individuals who envied her beauty, talent, intelligence, personality, signature style and charming character, to God in daily prayer. Prayer was the secret weapon of her survival. Had Mary Lou not learned who God was in her own life, she would have not been able to have the mindset that she maintained. That was one of the blessings that she clung to in times of bondage.

King James Bible

But my God shall supply all your needs according to his riches in glory by Christ Jesus.

Philippians 4:19

And it shall come to pass, that before they call, I will answer; and while they are yet speaking, I will hear. Isaiah 65:24

CHAPTER 5 PART 3
Blessings Beyond Bondage

Hugh, Mary Lou, Hubert, Marla and Michelle are in Cleveland, at Glenville SDA Church. We spent many Sabbaths at Glenville where Mary Lou's family and friends were members. Our family enjoyed the kind fellowship and great food at the home of Charles and Loreese Drake. Mrs. Drake was an awesome cook and made us feel right at home. Mrs. Ann Wooding was also a wonderful friend of Mary Lou who also shared great food and hospitality.

The ten plus years after Hugh's stroke and throughout his illness were grueling for Mary Lou at times. She was so involved with the progress of her family that she rarely had any time for relaxation. How she did everything is still a mystery because Mary Lou was not one to involve other people in her business. In conjunction with her privacy, she was extremely particular about whom she invited to her home.

Other than holidays and funerals, I can't think of any other times that Mary Lou was away from her job. She must have had one of the best attendance records of all the employees on her job. She had the same mindset about her children's attendance at school. Hubert and Marla were the only children receiving silver dollars for perfect attendance in some of the years that they were in elementary school. Mary Lou believed in giving the "old school remedies" like enemas and castor oil to keep her children in school. We all hated those home remedies, but loved every perfect attendance reward that we received.

During the years of 1964 through 1974, so many things rapidly took place. From 1964 to 66, Hugh was actively involved in regular physical rehabilitation. He spent long periods of hard work out sessions to strengthen his muscles and regain as much usage of his upper and lower body. On certain days he worked so hard that he only wanted to drive home to rest after leaving Toledo Hospital.

On other days Hugh would make several stops before going home. One of those stops was to his favorite mechanic, Chris, at *Dunkirk's Sunoco Filling Station*. Another stop would include *Slack's Barber Shop* where "Mr. Slack" would always have a huge smile to share for his friend, Hugh. Whether it was the Downtown Garden Store, a stop by Joseph's, A & P or Kroger's Supermarkets, people were always happy to see Hugh progressing from his therapy. The public community in Toledo, where he was well known, did not hesitate in encouraging Hugh.

On Sabbath, you could find Hugh climbing up the 13 concrete steps in front of the *Bethel SDA Church*. Every Sabbath he kept his focus and proceeded his challenging upward journey to the main sanctuary. Never deterred by weather or mood, Hugh Washington would not let his disability hold him back.

Even when some of the church members' sons would snicker and laugh while making fun of Hugh's inability to get to the restroom before having to urinate, my Father kept his dignity and self-worth in check. If those silly little boys had only known just how hard my Father worked in Physical Therapy, they would have never participated in such meanness. Yet, Daddy still kept on going, never choosing to stay home from church.

Hugh is wearing one of his silk signature ties, as he stands on the steps of Glenville SDA Church in Cleveland, Ohio. He did not let the many steps of Glenville keep him away from church attendance either.

Our Father had a deep reserve for keeping his mind on what was most important to him. That taught me a whole lot about the strength of Hugh Washington. His mindset was also strong and his love for God kept him climbing those 13 steps *every* Sabbath.

There was also so much to be said about the determination and dignity of Hugh Washington's mindset. He was definitely demonstrating his faith, courage and inner strength every time he faithfully climbed those "13 steps." One of Hugh's favorite hymns is found in the link. Listen to, "In Times Like These":

Listen to,

"In Times Like These":

https://youtu.be/y-Lcu-nspMA?si=xuXj1HCAZ_nuhXRG

Pictured above are the 13 concrete steps at Bethel SDA Church. Hugh Washington climbed them every Sabbath after surviving a paralyzing stroke.

This is a picture of The Bethel SDA Church in Toledo around 1955. Hubert is standing in the front row. He's the nearest boy not far from the wall. Mary Lou is not too far behind Hubert with the big hat that has white

netting in front.

Every Spring, Hugh planted a huge half acre vegetable garden on Clay Avenue. He had one of the best gardens in the Hyde Park Neighborhood. When the bondage of his illness cast shadows of darkness to promote depressive thoughts, then Hugh's garden gave him great satisfaction as well as a strong sense of accomplishment that all could behold throughout the summer.

For Mary Lou, Hugh's garden was a blessing to decrease their financial obligations and ease their tight budget. With all of the Native American gardening skills that he learned from David, his father, Hugh's corner garden was his pride and joy. The truest blessing of all was in the way the garden produced more than enough food for our family.

With the abundance of food, Mary Lou sent her children to "close by neighbors" to share free home grown vegetables with them. She did the same thing with surplus fruit from the yellow, Golden Delicious and Red Macintosh Apple Trees. Mary Lou found their Clay Avenue home to be a wonderful haven of financial support throughout this season of difficulty.

In addition to Hugh's garden, their land provided 2 peach trees, 1 dark plum tree, 5 apple trees, 1 dark Bing Cherry Tree, healthy Concord Grape Vines, 2 rhubarb patches, strawberry patches and raspberries to die for. On the weekends, Mary Lou would take time to can, multiple jars of applesauce for her winter cellar in the basement. She would also use some of the other fruits to make jellies and jams.

This is a Spring Picture of Mary Lou standing in the yard on Clay Avenue. In the background are the fruit trees that brought plentiful apples and Bing

Cherries during the summertime.

One of my most favorite memories of watching my Mother fulfill multiple roles was when she would come home from work, change her clothes, go directly to the garden and pick fresh vegetables to make her delicious vegetable gumbo for dinner. Mary Lou had her very own farmer's market right in her own yard. Although she had originally wanted to move out of the neighborhood, time had shown Mary Lou that God's providential plan had led her to yield to her husband's desire for reasons that she knew nothing about.

There were many places that they could have lived, but where would they have found so many of the natural resources that came with the affordable purchase price of their Clay Avenue Home? For the acre of land that accompanied their home, Hugh and Mary Lou received so many bonuses.

The variety of mature fruit trees, vines and beautiful flowers were like a paradise that few people could claim on their property. Even by today's realty standards, the more perks that come along with the land increases the value of that land.

In addition, my Mother's love for flowers was continuously fulfilled by the fragrant row of peony bushes, rose bushes and also her lilac tree. Mom was her own personal florist every time she went into the yard and cut from her own flowers to make arrangements. Often she would fill her personal vases and make her own arrangements to take to church on Sabbath. Once at church, she would place one of those freshly cut floral arrangements on top of the piano and the other one on the organ. That was how Mother found giving as natural as breathing air. It was her nature to do beautiful things so that others might experience joy, goodness and beauty.

God knew that Hugh would have a stroke. He also knew that Mary Lou would be hired by the housing authority which was 6 or 7 interstate exits away from Clay Avenue. All of these things were blessings in the midst of all the bondage.

Faithful Bethel SDA Members in Toledo (Left Picture): Left to Right: Blanche Owens, Ruth Lloyd, her daughter, Barbara Stevens and Marsha Tyson. Right Picture: First Elder, Elder Charles Wilson and his wife, Mrs. Wilson.

King James Bible

And all thy children shall be taught of the LORD;
and great shall be the peace of thy children.
Isaiah 54:13

CHAPTER 5 PART 4
Blessings Beyond Bondage

One of the definitions used to define bondage is "hardship". If any one word could be used to express the trend of Mary Lou's life, then hardship would be an accurate word. There was nothing truly ever easy about her journey even before her journey got started. But the greater the trial, the sweeter the triumph. That is what made freedom so sweet for the slaves. No matter what the oppression had been in the life of the slaves, once they had received the taste of freedom, they could truly appreciate the feeling of exuberance that came along with triumphantly overcoming their enslavement.

The blessings beyond the moments of bondage within Mary Lou's life were always moments of triumph. One of those moments was in 1966 when Hubert graduated from High School. (Pine Forge Academy)

In the collage above, Hubert is marching with Darlene Stowe from Bermuda. It is the Senior Class Presentation at Pine Forge, March of 1966. Hubert is also seen singing with "The Chapel Four Quartet" during his 1965-1966 school year at Pine Forge Academy.

From left to right are: Maurice Williams, Hubert Washington, Tyrone Turner and A. Dennis Brooks. They had a great sound that was as smooth as "The Breath of Life Quartet".

In the last picture, Hubert is standing with his then high school sweetheart and now current wife, the former Adrienne West, during their Senior Year Pine Forge Banquet.

Any of our graduations were huge triumphs for our Mother because she was educating three children in private, Christian Schools which required expensive monthly tuition payments. When Hubert graduated from Pine Forge with a zero balance, that was a great triumph for Mary Lou. Hugh's stroke occurred during Hubert's very first year at Pine Forge.

It was in the summer of 1963, Mary Lou and Hugh had been through one hardship after the next just trying to get Hubert into a Seventh-day Adventist High School. The *predominantly* Caucasian Adventist Boarding Academies that were closest to Toledo would not accept Hubert not only because he was Black, but also because he was *a black male.*

The fact that Hubert's other white classmates who he had graduated with, from Goff Memorial Jr. Academy received immediate acceptance letters to Adelphian and Mount Vernon, was an automatic indication that racism was the only reason for his rejection to both Seventh-day Adventist College Preparatory Schools.

Adelphian Academy was the closest Adventist Academy in Holly, Michigan and was only about two hours away from Toledo. Mount Vernon Academy was located in Mt. Vernon, Ohio near Columbus, Ohio. Hubert's rejection letters from both of those Adventist Academies outraged not only Mary Lou but maybe even more so, Hugh who had originally planned for his children to attend public schools.

To think that this kind of subtle racism was continuing to happen within the circles of Adventist Institutions was a diabolical deed to both of my parents, but especially to Hugh. No black man who is a real man wishes to see his son lose educational opportunities because of the asinine attitudes of societal stupidity that are known for historically kicking down the black man.

Even now as I am editing this book, I think about the George Floyd court case and feel the revisiting of my childhood when the Civil Rights Era was in full swing. My parents had dealt with the trauma that often comes with being "Black in America". There were constant brick walls surrounding the Civil Rights timeframe. Hugh didn't at all appreciate some of the leaders within his own denominational preference discriminating against his first born and only son.

However, Mary Lou would not be stopped. She always made lemonade out of the lemons that life gave her. When Hubert was rejected from both of the Academies within the Ohio and Michigan Adventist Conferences, she sent Hubert almost 500 miles away to Pennsylvania. Pine Forge was the closest African American Adventist Academy in location from Toledo.

At first, it was tremendous bondage for Mary Lou to send her firstborn child that far away from home at the pivotal age of *fifteen*. From his premature birth, and on throughout his formative years, Hubert had always been sheltered and protected by Mary Lou's "eagle eye". As a Mother who had spent tremendous attentiveness toward her firstborn and only son, having to send Hubert 500 miles away from home at 15, because of racial prejudice and rejection was cruel.

This collage gives some visual insight about how much Mary Lou attended to the needs of Hubert, her firstborn child and as she often called him, her "number one son". That 500 miles, Pine Forge distance, between Hubert, Hugh and Mary Lou was truly difficult.

Imagine having to send your fifteen year old 500 miles away from home to attend a SDA Boarding High School only because of racial and gender discrimination.

Racial quotas were the norm for some Seventh-day Adventists Academies and Universities before and during the Civil Rights Era. Pine Forge and Oakwood were havens of affirmation and acceptance for so many African American students.

Only her faith in God and her promise to God to give her children an Adventist, Christian Education would allow her to surrender to that kind of sacrifice. When Hubert completed the 3 years and graduated from Pine Forge without any debt and also without any scandal, Mary Lou felt grateful for God's grace toward that triumph.

Four years later in the summer of 1970 when Hubert graduated from Oakwood College, Mary Lou's alma mater in Huntsville, Alabama, she and Hugh were two of the proudest parents in America. Hubert's graduation was a milestone not only for him but also for Oakwood College. Mary Lou had petitioned Oakwood's President, Dr. Frank Hale, to have a summer graduation for the 10 graduates who had completed their requirements at the end of that summer. *(See additional information on page 268 to learn more about Dr. Frank Hale.)

This was something that Oakwood College had never ever done since its origin. It was not an issue for Mary Lou to approach Dr. Hale on behalf of her first born and only son. Because she felt that not only Hubert but also the other nine students deserved a summer ceremony, Mary Lou requested it to happen. Her request became a reality and since that time in 1970, there has not ever been another Oakwood Summer Graduation, that I know of to this 2022 date.

Mary Lou was comfortable sharing her requests with Dr. Hale. Hubert had worked for Dr. Hale as his *presidential messenger,* while being in college at Oakwood. Initially in this daily role, Hubert had done so much walking throughout the campus until Hubert's shoes were repeatedly wearing out. When Hubert's phone calls home often were about asking for new shoes, Mary Lou called Dr. Hale with a *parental plea* that something needed to be done because Hubert was needing shoes *too frequently.* In response to our Mother's phone call, Dr. Hale provided Hubert with a brand new bicycle for all of his campus deliveries throughout the remaining 4 years of being Dr. Hale's office messenger. Even many years later, after Hubert's Oakwood Graduation, Dr. Hale and Mary Lou shared laughter about the "shoe story" when they were reunited at various public events.

My Mother was not afraid or ashamed to ask anyone about anything if she knew that she was right in doing so. Her unashamedly persistent nature became even greater if she was pursuing something on behalf of her children. The education of Hubert, Marla and I were of absolute importance to our Mother. She **never** backed down to help us receive what we needed. Her tenaciously strong mindset was relentlessly consistent and without doubt. As her children, we were the fortunate ones because, we were the ones who benefited from *Mary Lou's Mindset.*

This picture was taken in the summer of 1970 at Hubert's Oakwood College Graduation. From left to right are Marla, Hubert, Mary Lou, Hugh and Michelle standing in front of Mary Lou. Hubert's High School and College Graduations were the "only" graduations that Hugh was able to attend for his three children. Though physically challenged, Hugh walked all over Oakwood's campus that weekend, never complaining and "as proud as a peacock" about Hubert's college graduation. Another highlight of that weekend was Hugh's reunion with Dr. Ernest Rogers. (Please see page 275 for additional information about Dr. Ernest Rogers) Dr. Rogers and Hugh had been childhood friends in Memphis, Tennessee. They had a wonderful time sharing "Memphis Memories". Please see link to learn more about Dr. Rogers:

https://www.youtube.com/watch?v=px5FUjiX1BM

Once again Hubert graduated from an Adventist Boarding Institution with a zero balance and a favored name. Hugh was so proud of his only son and firstborn child. His heart was filled with perfect joy because he had allowed his *"Bunny",* Mary Lou, to have her way with their children's educational journey. For a man who had only received the level of a High School diploma, Hugh Washington felt truly blessed beyond the bondage of his stroke. Once again, *Mary Lou's Mindset* had made a positive difference for those within her life. In addition, with her spirit of giving, she allowed the **excess credit balance on Hubert's Oakwood Account** to be given and credited to an incoming student's account who was going to be an Oakwood Freshman in the Fall of 1970.

While Mary Lou was celebrating the completion of one child's educational journey, she was back at square one with the process of sending another child off to Academy. This time, Mary Lou would not accept the bigotry and inequalities that she had been faced with in 1963. She would not allow the bondage from others' shallow mindsets to block the blessings that she knew rightfully belonged to her daughter Marla.

Marla was the President and Valedictorian of her eighth grade class at the Toledo Seventh-day Adventist Church School. (Formerly named Goff Memorial Jr Academy). Mary Lou was not expecting the same rejection letter to come from Adelphian Academy after Marla applied for entrance in 1970. But cruelty still had a face within the educational realm of Adventist Institutions that were owned and operated by some Caucasian Conferences.

It was unfortunate that after all that history had been revealed through televised accounts of the Civil Rights Era, that any denominational church school could still remain comfortably incorrect with the subtlety of rejecting students because of race and skin color. The deeper misfortune was that it was occurring under the denominational umbrella of the Seventh-day Adventist Church in which Mary Lou and Hugh were both raised throughout their childhoods.

This truly scorned Hugh, while it outraged Mary Lou. You could not ever mess with Mary Lou's children and get away with it, especially when they were on the side of right. My Mother was worse than a "Mother Grizzly" if she knew you had mistreated her 3 children. The worst part for the offenders was that Mary Lou had no hesitation at all to immediately confront and document anyone who involved themselves with any kind of harm to Hubert, Marla and Michelle.

When the Adelphian Academy Admissions Committee decided to send a rejection letter to Marla in 1970, *Mary Lou's Mindset* relentlessly went into a form of activism that would not accept any standard of bondage. In the summer of 1970, my Mother sent letters, made phone calls, personally confronted and consistently communicated her disbelief, dissatisfaction and disgust concerning the discrimination that was once again being used against one of her children.

Mary Lou even politely shared her story with Elder Wernick, who was the Lake Union Conference President that presided over all of the Adventist Churches and Schools within the states of Wisconsin, Illinois, Indiana and Michigan. Without any hesitation, Mary Lou caught Elder Wernick as he was coming off the platform at the

Lake Region Conference Camp Meeting, in the summer of 1970. She introduced herself and immediately started informing him about Marla's rejection letter.

He uncomfortably listened and said he would get back to her from his office the following week. But informing the Lake Union President about Marla's rejection from Adelphian Academy was not enough for him to make the difference. Inadequate excuses were given to Mary Lou about Marla being an out of state resident. Still our Mother would not accept the responses that she was receiving that were only *curtains of disguise* to block the real issues of keeping color quotas for black students.

Mary Lou knew that once again Marla was not receiving a letter of acceptance for the same reason that Hubert had not received his acceptance letter back in 1963. However, this time, Mary Lou *would not* accept the same rejection without a fight. She continued on her journey of justice without blinking one eye and went all the way to the top of the Adventist level, the General Conference. It was as if she could not and would not be moved. And with the same boldness that Pearl had told the criminals at her back door that she would blow their heads off, Mary Lou courageously sat down and prepared a letter to the President of the General Conference, Elder Neal Wilson.

Her determination and faith was as persistent as that of Mary Louise when she refused to let Ethel Waters raise Mary Lou. Mary Louise wouldn't change her decision and now Mary Lou was not about to back away from the position of standing up for her daughter's rights. That kind of courageous determination seemed like it was natural to Mary Lou when one took the time to stop and consider the bold persistence of Pearl and Mary Louise. Mary Lou had been taught resilience from the very best warriors. She had learned first-hand from Mary Louise about how prayer could be a weapon of defense when an individual firmly put their trust in the promises of the Lord.

With that being said, Mary Lou did not feel defeated after Elder Wernick's letter of shameful inequality. She propelled her energy and writing skills onward to President Neal Wilson's office and never looked back. After Mary Lou wrote one of her most prolific letters to President Neal Wilson, who was at that time the President of the Seventh-day Adventist Church World Headquarters in Washington D.C., Marla received an automatic acceptance letter within very little time.

In 1973, when Marla graduated from Adelphian, she did so with honors. She also did so with the accomplishment of being the first African American to graduate within a 3-year period, under an accelerated curriculum that was composed of the same credit hours required for the 4-year college preparatory diploma. As one of the 1973 Bell Echoes Editor of her senior yearbook, Marla shared her keen intelligence, impeccable details and superior skill to make sure that album of memories would represent her classmates in a remarkable way.

As a Mother, Mary Lou could not have been any prouder of Marla's successful standards. My Mother was glowing with gratitude over the way her prayers had been victoriously answered throughout the duration of Marla's academy days. Though the summer struggle of 1970 had been a continual uphill battle, the end blessing was like a double rainbow at the end of a storm tossed tornado.

God had given Mary Lou and Marla an ending of triumphant excellence that exceeded all expectations of racial prejudice. Once again, God had guided Mary Lou to help blaze a trail beyond racial discrimination. Whatever achievements Hubert, Marla, or I ever received throughout our lives were based upon the foundational years that our Mother laid to guide and prepare us for our futures. We would have never reached any of the plateaus that we gained had it not been for the determination, courage and faith in God that Mary Lou's Mindset held for each of her three children. With her tenacious mindset, our Mother held firm to God's Will.

Marla Washington

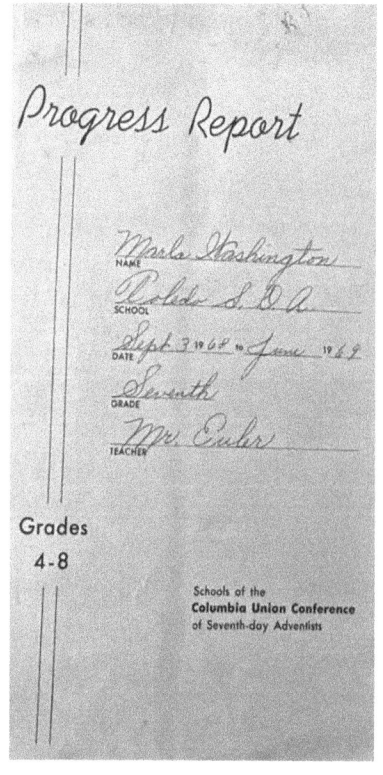

Scholarship Record

	PERIOD				
	1	2	3	4	Final Grade
ARITHMETIC	B-	B	B-	C+	B
ART	B-	B+	B+	A	B+
BIBLE	A	A	A	A	A
LANGUAGE ARTS:					
English	B+	A	B+	A	A
Handwriting	B+	B-	B-	A	B+
Reading	B-	B-	B-	B	B
Spelling	A-	A	A	A	A
HEALTH "LIVING"	A-	A-	A	A	A
MUSIC	B	B	A-	A	B+
SCIENCE					
SOCIAL STUDIES:					
Geography	B	B+	B-	A	B+
United States History					
State History	B	A		A	
PRACTICAL ARTS ( )					
PHYSICAL EDUCATION	A	A	A	A	A

KEY TO MARKING

A—Excellent work
B—Very good work
C—Average work
D—Below average work
F—Below passing in effort and work

Citizenship Record

No mark means satisfactory. (N) indicates a weakness and a need to improve.

	PERIOD			
	1	2	3	4
HABITS AND ATTITUDES				
1. Is cheerful				
2. Is courteous in speech and action				
3. Shows a spirit of reverence				
4. Is cooperative				
WORK HABITS				
1. Uses time wisely				
2. Works independently				
3. Works well with others				
4. Takes pride in neat work				
5. Completes tasks promptly				
6. Follows directions				
7. Carries responsibility				
SOCIAL HABITS				
1. Uses self control				
2. Participates in play activities				
3. Plays well with others				
4. Respects personal and public property				
5. Helps to keep school neat and clean				
6. Observes safety rules				

Attendance Record

	1	2	3	4
Days Present	41	50	45	
Days Absent	0	0	0	0
Times Tardy	0	0	0	0

Dear Parents:

To help your child succeed:

1. Have family worship and pray with your child daily.
2. Send him to school regularly.
3. Send him on time.
4. See that he gets 8 to 10 hours sleep every night.
5. Provide a well-balanced diet.
6. Encourage cleanliness.
7. Have physical defects corrected.
8. Encourage him to do his best and praise him for his effort and progress.
9. Consult the teacher if any question arises about your child's progress.

Secretary of Education
Columbia Union Conference
7710 Carroll Avenue
Takoma Park, Maryland 20012

PARENT'S SIGNATURE

First Report *Mrs. M. L. Washington*

Second Report *Mrs. M. L. Washington*

Third Report *Mrs. M. L. Washington*

CLASSIFICATION FOR NEXT YEAR

Your child's classification for next year is based on his physical, mental, and social development. It is recommended that

he be { promoted to / ~~assigned to~~ / ~~retained in~~ } grade 8 for the

1969-1970 school year.

Teacher *L. G. Euler*

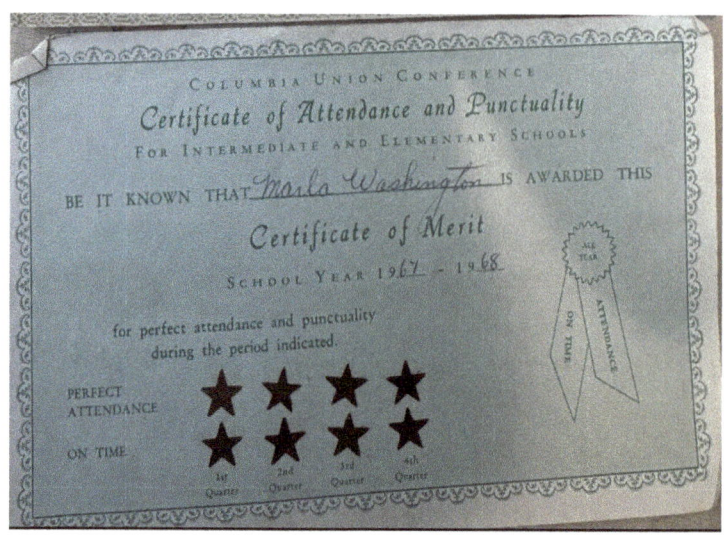

On pages 148, 149, & 150 are Marla's documents in the following order: Seventh Grade Report Card, Perfect Attendance Certificate 1967-68 and last 8/12/1977 Speech & Hearing Ohio License.

Had it not been for our Mother's loving faithfulness to God and her children, the successful outcomes would not have ever been attained. Mary Lou proved the words of President Abraham Lincoln to be true. His quote says, "All that I am or hope to be, I owe to my angel Mother." For Hubert, Marla and Michelle this quote has been a reality within their lives. The earnest prayers of our Mother have forever covered our lives.

King James Bible

Her children arise up, and call her blessed; her husband also, and he praiseth her.

Proverbs 31:28

CHAPTER 5 PART 5
Blessings Beyond Bondage

Life has a way of teaching you lessons that you never signed up to take. In the final analysis of it all, one may find that their greatest daily life experiences are the very things that are preparing them for some greater future opportunity. Such was the case for Mary Lou. All along the twists and turns of her journey, were future avenues that would often bring her outcomes of joy.

Life in Toledo had certainly not been the most pleasant. From the beginning of her arrival to Hugh's hometown, Mary Lou was the center of attention at his boyhood church and also his boyhood neighborhood. At church, there were old girlfriends that were not happy about Mary Lou marrying their admired hometown bachelor. They gave her the glare of envy each week as she came dressed like a model from head to toe. Mary Lou's beauty was not her only point of being envied. Her wardrobe had been well stocked by her older sisters who lived in California and worked for wealthy employers.

As Aunt Hazel explained,

"Some of the folk that Cassie and I worked for were very rich. They had plenty of money to buy beautiful clothes. They knew we had a sister who was going to college in Alabama so they would give us gorgeous clothes that they no longer wanted. Most of the time they had only worn those things one time and a lot of times the clothes were brand new with the tags still on them. They just bought them and decided they didn't want them when they got home. Cassie and I would put those things together and send Mary Lou boxes of beautiful clothes whenever we could."

In this photo, Mary Lou is sitting in the front and center (second right) with a fresh flower on the side of her hair on the lawn of Oakwood's Campus. She is with the club that the renown, Dr. Eva B. Dykes sponsored and mentored. It is very probable that Mary Lou's gown was sent to her from California from either of her sisters, Hazel or Cassie.

(Please see page 265 to learn more about Dr. Dykes.)

https://www.youtube.com/watch?v=G36KbSvf2YU

This is a picture of Mary Lou with 3 of her 5 sisters. They are standing in birth order. From left to right is Daisy, Hazel, Cassie and Mary Lou on the right end. Aunt Hazel and Aunt Cassie were the sisters that sent Mary Lou her wardrobe from wealthy employers that they worked for in Los Angeles. Aunt Daisy was a professional seamstress in Detroit, Michigan. Between these 3 sisters, Mary Lou had a wardrobe fit for a queen during her Oakwood College days and even afterwards. They loved keeping their "little sister" very well stocked with a wonderful wardrobe.

This sisterly blessing was so wonderful that it made some of Mary Lou's college classmates who were not from Cleveland think that she had come from a family that had financial prosperity. Between her ability to sew her own clothes and also her oldest sister Daisy, who was a professional seamstress and lived only 60 miles away from Toledo, near Detroit, Mary Lou's wardrobe was truly the desire of *any* woman. For over an entire year, as a newlywed, Mary Lou wore a different outfit to church without repeating anything from her closet. It disturbed one of the church ladies so bad until she approached Mary Lou after church and remarked,

"I wondered when you were going to break your cycle of different outfits. I noticed that you wore something different every Sabbath for over the whole year since you've been here."

That totally surprised Mary Lou. The fact that one of the church members had watched Mary Lou so closely about something that was always normal for her to do, really surprised her.

She had not been keeping track of what she was wearing. Mary Lou was just enjoying being well groomed because she always tried to look her very best. As she shared her musical gifts of playing the piano, the organ and singing, Mary Lou added fuel to the fire for those who were insecure about Hugh's new bride. My Mother was not a vain woman. She always had a secret inner conflict with herself because of the fact that Pearl had given her away.

It always amazed me that my Mother saw herself as being ordinary. She did not see herself as beautiful as she was considered to be by her admirers and spectators.

In the late 1980s, one of my Mother's Oakwood classmates asked me, *"You are Mary Lou Battle's daughter? Your Mother was one of the prettiest girls on Oakwood's Campus when we were in school as classmates."*

Mary Lou is seated taking this picture while part of a wedding party of her friends in Cleveland. She was engaged to Hugh at the time. The simplicity of her beauty radiates the elegance of her graceful style. How could she not realize the full measure of her natural beauty?

When I later called my Mom and shared those comments with her, she laughed and then said,

"I didn't feel that way. There were other girls that I felt were prettier than me."

That response indicated to me that my Mother did not truly see herself for all that she truly was.

Her focus had not been on the things that most would have first considered as most valuable, because Mary Lou was always on her mission of reaching her goals and aiming for the very best that she could receive. In that sense she was very unique because she did not care about using her beauty to gain promotion or power.

The fact that she was uninterested in approaching Hugh on that first Saturday, when he came to her childhood church, told much about Mary Lou's focus and humble character. As so often many women do, Mary Lou, to the contrary, did not have an inner need to use her beauty for gain.

During the 30 years that Mary Lou lived in Toledo, she learned to live an even more self-reliant life. By the time of Hugh's death in 1974, Mary Lou had almost perfected the valuable life lesson of being your own woman no matter what. Through her ever winding journey of being a dedicated wife to Hugh and in also being a dedicated Mother to her children, Mary Lou had found that her twenties, thirties, forties and beginning fifties were what she had determined they could be because of her dependence on God.

In the fall of 1972, when Hugh's health began to plummet, Mary Lou had to reach deep down within herself to make decisions that she knew would be criticized. It was unsafe for Hugh to continue to remain at home without assistance during the work day. For this reason, Mary Lou placed him at the Parkview Nursing and Rehabilitation Center. For that one decision, Mary Lou was rebuked by those who had always needed an opportunity to find fault with her character. When the exorbitant costs from Parkview's bills surpassed the financial abilities of the family budget, Mary Lou was again faced with new choices.

She reached out to Mr. Espie Carter, an Adventist nursing home administrator in Oberlin, Ohio. Brother Carter, as church folk called him, owned a nursing facility that had a good reputation within his community. When Mary Lou spoke to him about placing Hugh there, he was like an angel sent from Heaven. Brother Carter had a great compassion for Mary Lou's hardship.

He saw her dual sincerity to insure that her spouse received quality healthcare while also providing her children with a quality Christian Education. Because of his compassionate spirit, Brother Carter worked out a financial arrangement that could meet Hugh's insurance coverage and Mary Lou's budget.

This is a picture of Mr. Espie Carter, Owner & Administrator of *Carter's Nursing Home* in Oberlin, Ohio. Mr. Carter was a member of the Oberlin SDA Church and he was married to Bessie Carter, who Carter Hall (Oakwood Women's Dormitory) is named after. See the link for more information: https://www.youtube.com/watch?v=9zS8H3P_rfk

On the right, in next picture, Mary Lou is standing as Residence Dean of Carter Hall with Dean Dorothy Holloway. Ironically, Mary Lou served as a Dean in Carter Hall and also lived in the Dean's Apartment there.

Once Hugh was moved to Carter's Nursing Home, Mary Lou became the center of increased criticism. Those who had always been jealous and had never wanted to accept her as Hugh's wife, took this time to extend their negative church gossip even further. For my Mother it was a time of increased difficulty.

Every other weekend as the weather permitted, Mary Lou drove with Marla and I, on Fridays after work, to see Hugh. It was an additional strain upon her because she was already over extended just trying to keep up with the school requirements that Marla and I had, as well as the requirements from her job. Oberlin was almost two hours away from Toledo. The driving alone took its toll on Mary Lou every time we traveled to Oberlin.

While in Oberlin, we stayed at our Cousin's, Cleo Battle-Dawson's home. Cousin Cleo was so gracious to our family. She was the perfect hostess and one of the best cooks in the entire Battle Family. Her home was a haven of comfort for us at a time when we were transitioning to the details of our Father's nursing home relocation. Cousin Cleo made it easier.

Hubert married in December of 1972 so he was focused upon the journey of being a newlywed and attentive new husband. His wedding was at the Oberlin Church on Park Street. It was held there just so our Father could be in attendance. That was the last time Daddy came out to a public event. Two years later, in December of 1974, Hugh Washington passed away.

Washington Family Portrait at Hubert's Wedding in December 1972. It was the last family portrait we ever took. Hugh died in December of 1974. Photography Credits Lucian Dixon

The old religious song says,

"If it had not been for the Lord on my side, where would I be, where would I be?"

That song should have been Mary Lou's theme song because it was only God's goodness on her behalf that pulled her through not only the bondage but all of the opposition that some used to try to make her already hard journey even harder. In a strange way, it seemed that all she had learned to overcome in Cleveland and at Oakwood, groomed her for the trials in Toledo.

Although often mistreated, Mary Lou did not wallow in self-pity. Neither did she allow her kindness to be paralyzed by the unkind actions of her offenders. Our Mother would distance herself from those who deliberately used her and she'd also make their unkind actions a matter of prayer. Mary Lou did not want her blessings to be withheld because of her own actions. For that reason, she tried to stay on the proverbial "high road".

After Hugh's death in December of 1974, Mary Lou focused even more heavily upon Marla and Michelle. Marla was studying at Toledo University to receive dual degrees in Speech & Hearing and also Education. Marla had pleaded with Mary Lou to allow her the opportunity to stay at home to receive her College Degrees. Though it was directly in opposition to Mary Lou's commitment to Christian Education and having all of her children attend Oakwood College, Mary Lou gave in to Marla's request and allowed her to study in Toledo. One of the major reasons Mary Lou decided this was because Oakwood did not offer a degree in Speech and Hearing.

Being the Mother that Mary Lou was, she decided to seek the help of Mr. Art Edgerton who was married to one of Hugh and Mary Lou's former neighbors. Della Edgerton readily invited Mary Lou and Marla to come to their home and meet her husband, Art.

Mr. Edgerton was well known in Toledo because he had his own television program on the CBS affiliate station, WTOL. He was an articulate and talented black man whose blindness did not make any difference in regards to his accomplishments. Art Edgerton was the Ray Charles of Toledo. He could sing and make an organ jump. *(See U. S. Congressional Notice on page 266)*

The second picture is a photo of Marla during the time of her collegiate days of studying Speech & Hearing and also Education at The University of Toledo. She maintained her required grades throughout her coursework and retained her Martin Luther King Scholarship (which included free textbooks), during her entire 4 years (1973-1977) of attending "T. U." and until her graduation. On the top of her 1977 Graduation Cap, Marla had attached gold adhesive letters that said, "Thank You, Jesus." They could be seen from the seats throughout the arena. Photo Credit: Kmart Promotional Photography

The press photo above shows Art Edgerton receiving The United States 1967 Handicapped of the Year Award. He was awarded by Vice President, Hubert Humphrey. See pages 266 & 267 for additional information and credits about this.

When he met Marla, he was fascinated with her story and how she had tenaciously handled racism in her young, teenage life. After listening to her educational desires and career goals to become a speech therapist, Art Edgerton made a couple of phone calls and directed Mary Lou and Marla to the University of Toledo. It was there that she applied for the Dr. Martin Luther King Jr. Scholarship.

The rest was history. Marla entered college at "T. U." on that full scholarship that paid for everything, including her books. Mary Lou did not have to make any tuition payments for Marla's *entire* college education. That financial blessing was one that God had led Mary Lou to just by thinking about her friendship with Della Edgerton when Della (then Della Collins) formerly lived within the Hyde Park neighborhood.

Mary Lou's kindness to others was often returned to her in ways that she never expected. Whenever my Mother was extending her kindness to individuals who had not been kind to her, she would simply explain her actions by saying,

"All that you send into the lives of others comes back into your own."

When it came to sending goodness into her children's lives, Mary Lou poured an enormous amount of wisdom into each of our minds. Mother made sure that we would have more than she ever had. She encouraged us to all get a college education at Oakwood, her alma mater.

Mary Lou was absolutely thrilled when all of us received our college degrees. When Marla received her Master's Degree in Speech and Hearing Therapy from The University of Alabama A & M, our Mother attended and rejoiced. It was because of the directives and advice of Dr. Nell (Rice) Anthony, which she shared with Mary Lou, that Marla was able to enroll and receive *total financial support* from a grant for her Master's at *Alabama A&M University. For that reason, Marla received a tuition free Master's Degree in Speech and Hearing.*

Mary Lou's encouragement concerning any of her children's goals was always available. Even when I came short, by "only three tests" of not being able to return to school before the time limits of completing the requirements for my Master's degree in Elementary Counseling, my Mother still found words of encouragement for me. She said,

"Michelle, if you never get a Master's Degree, just always remember that you have done enough hard work and helped more than enough children all over this country to equal that of receiving a Doctorate Degree."

We both shared a big laugh that day because we both knew just how much hard work I had done during my career as a Teacher, an Educator and also as a Principal.

Even more so, it was my Mother who had known all about my educational journey from its very beginning in first grade. She had been the relentless motivator that had pushed behind me when I refused to speak for the first 3 months upon entering school. Yes, for 3 entire months, I was mute within my classroom only communicating by using my head to shake up and down for "yes" and left and right for "no".

Every night Mary Lou would come home from work, prepare dinner, and then transition to the telephone where she would call Mrs. Patricia Geach, my First Grade Teacher to find out what I had not finished in class on that particular day. At times I could see that my Mother was "beyond frustrated" with my withdrawal at school.

One night she looked at me and said,

"Michelle, why won't you talk and do your work in school when you come home and talk and finish everything Mrs. Geach gives you in class?"

Although those three months were "added weight" upon my Mother's already overloaded responsibilities, she **never** gave up on me and **neither did** Mrs. Geach. Had it not been for the prayerful faith, determination, and consistency that she and Mrs. Geach had in God while working with me, I probably would have been sent back home to enter school the following year. Because of the tenacious spirit of both my Mother and Mrs. Geach, as well as their belief that I could and would evolve, I pulled through first grade successfully as one of the top readers in the class. That was the faith of Mary Lou. She would not release her hopes in God's purpose for her children.

Our Mother had always been our biggest cheerleader and she left no stone unturned while making sure that all three of us got a private, Christian Education, as well as our college degrees. How many Mothers of 3 children and a husband with disabilities, operating with *"one salary"*, can claim that story? The words of a favorite old hymn say, *" It is no secret what God can do. What He's done for others He will do for you."* For Mary Lou and her family, that old hymn was more than a reality within their lives.

No matter what the challenge was, *Mary Lou's Mindset* arose to practice the determination, courage and faith that it had known in times before. Implementing what Mary Lou knew was effectively sound was a way of life for her, because Mary Lou found a resting place within the dependability of a never failing God. Although surrounded by constant difficulties which could have been viewed as impassable barriers, our Mother chose to keep her daily mindset fixed upon the Heavenly Promise Keeper who never disappoints.

Often our Mother would prayerfully revisit the family budget to fulfill new financial emergencies or needs that arose. Her mindset of *"God will provide"* was her concrete belief system. She was as diligent to the management of her household finances as she was to those that she was accountable for at *TMHA* (Toledo Metro Housing Authority). The financial mentoring that she exemplified was beyond reproach. As she kept the upstairs fireproof home safe like an armored treasury of legal documents and paperwork, Mary Lou systematically accounted for everything she deemed important within that chosen closet of safe keeping. Even Hubert, Marla and Michelle's report cards were filed within that safe. Our Mother's accountability was unforgettable. Maybe that's one of the reasons that she was the church clerk for 12 successive years at Bethel SDA Church in Toledo.

God had given Mary Lou many talents and she did not mind using them for His honor and glory. Her loyal faithfulness to working for the Lord within her church and denomination was ever true.

This is the class photo of my First Grade Class. Mrs. Geach is top and center. I am on the right end of the third row, with two bows on top of both braids.

Mary Lou was a working Mother who made time to do "two thick heads of hair" for school. Marla (on the right side picture) was in fourth or fifth grade as seen above.

Occasionally, our Mother would purchase identical dresses for Marla and I to dress like twins. This picture was one of those times. We were the center of conversation whenever we wore matching outfits.

This is a group photo of my very first class in Brooklyn, New York. (Autumn 1982) Those 27 second graders at the Hanson Place S.D.A. School gave me the best experience for my teaching career. Mrs. Geach and my Mother's persistence paid off "16 years" later. Both of them taught me the wonderful power of how believing in "God's purpose for a child" can make a tremendous difference.

The class photo above was of my second year of teaching in Brooklyn. This was the class that I left when I resigned (in winter of 1984) and moved to Fontana, California to take care of my 92 year old grandfather, Elder David Washington. I hated to leave them however, after deep prayer and fasting, I had to follow what God was leading me to do. It was a great blessing to be with my "Gramps" during the closing stages of his life. He was truly a God fearing Man of God who had been a colporteur during The Great Depression.

The collage above shows pictures of Hubert and Michelle's Oakwood College Graduations in 1970 and 1982. Marla's Alabama A &M University Graduation when Marla received her Master's Degree is also shown. This collage also holds 2 pictures of Mary Lou in her 1947 Oakwood College Graduation photo (top) as well as the photo of her in 1988 (bottom), when she received an Honorary Doctorate in Birmingham.

The bottom left picture includes Dr. Calvin Rock, 8th. President of Oakwood. President Rock was the son-in-law of President Frank L. Peterson who had been Mary Lou's Oakwood President. His wife Clara (Peterson) Rock,(who passed away in June of 2018) was the developer and First Archivist of The Eva B. Dykes Library at Oakwood during my Oakwood enrollment.

Dr.B. Baker Interview with Dr. Rock: *https://youtu.be/1DT5OaN0Zuc?si=ly-NrjfMi2B1gtl3*

At all of our graduations, I believe that Mary Lou was one of the happiest Mothers on Planet Earth. It was one of the heights of Mary Lou's Motherhood to see all of her children graduate from college. Education was the key to independence and financial security. Ensuring that her children had their degrees meant that they could have better opportunities for stability in their lives. Mary Lou pushed all three of her children to reach their highest potential. With her *Mindset of Faith*, she would never be easily discouraged when it came to any of the goals that she set and prayed over. Her faith in God's promises was the hope that Mary Lou focused upon throughout her toughest challenges.

At times it seemed *financially unattainable* for Mary Lou to pay tuition for *three* children who were attending Seventh-day Adventist elementary schools, Adelphian and Pine Forge Academies and eventually Oakwood College. Yet it was her vow to fulfill the guidance of God's Word for her children. *"All thy children shall be taught of the Lord and great shall be the peace of thy children."* (Isaiah 54:13) *Having* the blessing of experiencing the fulfillment of that vow was *total joy* for our Mother. Giving her children the full matriculation of Adventist Education and having them receive diplomas from Seventh-day Adventist Institutions was more than she had received. Then lastly, to have witnessed all of her 3 adult children serve as educators was also something that our Mother was gratefully proud and thankful for.

As the last born of Mary Lou's children, after my Oakwood Graduation, I had the privilege of watching her no longer live on the constraints of struggling to meet the responsibilities of Adventist tuition payments. For so many years she had lived with very strict financial standards, especially when Hugh was a stroke patient.

Our family would never have made it through those tough times had it not been for the thrifty mindset of Mary Lou. Her faithfulness to return her tithe and offerings was always at the foundation of her financial giving. After that, she had a systematic way of keeping track of all the monthly finances and household obligations. In the scheme of it all, I will never forget how earnestly she protected her pristine credit score. Even in her eighties, after moving off the Oakwood Campus and when she applied for her only apartment in Huntsville, her over 700 credit score went through for approval within a few minutes. Mr. Paul Foster, one of the Oakwood Accountants, once told Mary Lou,

"Dean, I can tell when it's the first of the month whenever I see you coming to the office."

That was the character of our "business minded" Mother. She believed in living **debt free** as much as possible and she would often remind us of how she had been raised to be content with the blessings that God had given.

Mary Lou was proud of her children becoming 3 educators. Pictured above, Hubert was serving as a Teacher Principal at the Avondale Adventist School in Chattanooga. Marla was serving as a Speech Therapist for Nashville Metro Schools, and I was serving in Birmingham at Ephesus Academy as the Grade 2 Teacher.

New International Version of the Bible

10 A wife of noble character who can find?
   She is worth far more than rubies.
11 Her husband has full confidence in her
   and lacks nothing of value.
12 She brings him good, not harm,
   all the days of her life. Proverbs 31:10-12

CHAPTER 5 PART 6
Blessings Beyond Bondage

If Mary Lou's Mindset was part of the strength that helped her triumph, what would the outcome be if her strong will found a path of unexpected diversion?

In the summer of 1975 she would begin a new journey that would change the course of her well known routines that she had kept so consistently. After Hugh's death, some of the men who had admired Mary Lou throughout Hugh's illness, stepped forward to make their intentions known. Because they had observed Mary Lou's faithful commitment to our father during his illness, those who were secret spectators were eager to approach Mary Lou for courtship.

I was 3 years old when my father had his stroke. At the time of his death, I was 14. Being a "Daddy's Girl" from the time of my toddler days made his sickness and death a true hardship for me. I loved my Mother dearly, but it was "Daddy" that had my heartstrings.

This is a photo of my Dad introducing "the new family puppy" to me.
Our father was happy to provide loving gifts for our family. He was pleased to provide his wife and their 3 children with loving surprises.

From the onset of my Father's illness and even before, I had been his shadow. My preschool days were spent accompanying him everywhere he went Monday through Friday. I was never ashamed of my Father because he was physically disabled.

On the contrary, I was totally ashamed of those shallow individuals who only saw his physical challenges and inability due to the paralyzing effects from his stroke. I know that some children can often be cruel toward different individuals when they have not been taught or exposed to those who have disabilities. However, it never sat well with me that some of the boys who attended our church were the worst ones to mock my Dad's physical impairments.

My Father was truly a fighter in every sense of the word. He had not sat down and given up after his stroke. He fought to regain his physical strength and he also fought to be able to drive again. Hugh Washington made sure that he would be behind the wheel. After all, that is how he had spent 22 years of his career. For my Father, driving was not just an optional goal of his physical therapy. Driving was the main goal of his physical therapy.

I cannot imagine just how traumatized Hugh must have been to be in a physically disabled state. One day he was up walking, driving, simonizing his personal car, playing with his children and fulfilling any needs that pertained to his family. Then the next day he was in the hospital being told that he was paralyzed by a stroke and disabled from working. How extremely variant are the spectrums of those two scenarios. For my father, his disability was like an unbelievable deep valley. It seemed at times that there was no ending to that seemingly bottomless pit.

As the youngest of my siblings, I often felt the depth of that dark psychological tunnel that barricaded my father's former freedom from being the man that he had once so happily been.

Hugh Washington was a man who needed no one's earthly permission to live in his own skin. For him to have to answer to the dictates of medical doctors, physical therapists and medical specialists assigned to his care was beyond humbling for Hugh. Yet "Hugh David", as Mary Lou would at times call him, gave in to what he had to do for the benefit of his health recovery.

If I could have done anything to change the day that my Dad had his stroke, I surely would have quickly done so. The difficult life lessons that I learned in my life from between 3 and 14 years of age, about having a disabled parent, were unforgettably tough and cold. On so many days I was a first-hand witness about how intolerant individuals could be about physically challenged and disabled people. Some of the children of the 1960's and 70's were even more uneducated about tolerance for the disabled. Some of those children of such intolerance had no apparent remorse to stare, whisper, laugh and make critical fun of my father's physical inabilities.

As an overweight and shy child, I struggled with this kind of covert bullying. To see how insensitive some could be concerning my Dad's illness was a battle that I could not ever win, because it was done by sly individuals who were careful to not be seen or heard.

For me, it was *total trauma,* because my father was fighting a daily battle of withstanding all of his health hurdles, as well as holding on to his physical manhood that was slipping away because of his illness.

Hugh Washington was a loving, doting and intentionally committed Father. He did not want anything but true happiness for his children and he worked hard every day of his 5-day work week to provide the things that his children needed and wanted. Even in his illness, with all of the challenges that come from being a stroke survivor, Hugh gave life his best effort to remain the man that he had always been.

Hugh was so disheartened that illness had taken a strike at his health during the prime of his life. There were days when Hugh cried silent tears while spending times of personal retreat within the outdoor areas of his acreage. He knew that he would not be around to communicate his desires for his daughters' future suitors. As his health declined, Hugh also knew that he would not be alive to attend their college graduations and eventually their expectant weddings. Hugh would not have the joy of holding his newborn grandchildren while helping Mary Lou on the journey of lovingly spoiling them.

The photo above shows Mary Lou visiting with Hubert and his family in Rochester, New York. From left to right is Danielle Nicole, Hubert's daughter and Mary Lou's first born grandchild. Holding Danielle is Evelyn, Hubert's first wife. Hubert and Mary Lou are at the end. At the time, Hubert was the Fifth Grade Teacher at Rochester Jr. Academy which at that time was under the supervision of the New York Conference. Mary Lou had her Grandchildren call her "Nana". She was proud of Hubert and Marla's children and loved them all dearly.

Hugh had to come to terms with many things before his death. Those realities could not have been easy at all for a man who loved and adored his wife and children. Even harder must have been the fact that his "Bunny" would be biblically free to be pursued for marriage after his death. Looking back, now that I have passed the season of my Father's age, at the time of his death, I can truly say that what his mind may have reviewed was totally bondage.

Leroy Hemingway had never forgotten the unforeseen moves that Hugh had made to marry Mary Lou. In fact, Leroy made a visit with his second wife to see Hugh and Mary Lou on Clay Avenue several years earlier. He acted as though he was perfectly over the fact that Hugh had beat him out to the girl of his boastful dreams. But that was only an act.

While Mary Lou and Marla were attending a wedding in Cleveland in the summer of 1976, who should walk up and approach both of them but Leroy Hemingway. Divorced and supposedly visiting his Mother while on vacation, Leroy coincidentally dropped by the wedding to see old childhood friends that he knew from growing up in Cleveland. That was his platform and Mary Lou was his prey.

Like a sly fox watching the chicken coop, Leroy made intentional moves towards Mary Lou, calculating how he could also impress Marla who was in the prime of her life and near the age that Mary Lou had been when he had so admired Mary Lou in days of long ago. Before the reception was over, Leroy had accomplished his mission.

He had left such an impression upon Marla until she could not stop from talking about him when she and Mary Lou got back to Toledo later that night. It was the moment that changed the rest of all of our lives because Leroy and Mary Lou were married before the summer of 1976 ended.

Leroy Hemingway was an intelligent man whose calculating schemes were well polished by a lifetime of deception. For every lie that he told, he had an amazing story to make it seem as though he was being totally transparent. Within the first year of their marriage, Leroy told so many lies to so many of my Mother's family, friends, neighbors and church members until his lies were like a growing lottery whose numbers were undrawn. The worst part about his lies is that almost everyone believed them. This was the cunning weaponry that he used to gain power within the social and familial circles of Mary Lou's life.

The worst bondage that ever occurred within Mary Lou's, Marla's and Michelle's life was due to Mary Lou's marriage to Leroy Hemingway. Like a no good scoundrel, he perpetrated every lie that he could to benefit from every "no good agenda" that was hidden in his wicked heart. By the time Mary Lou divorced Leroy in 1987, he had left suffering and scars from the Satanic Warfare that had come from his demonic actions. The fact that he had become a practicing Adventist Pastor with all of the rights, privileges and credentials, made his masquerades of mistaken identity more potent.

He used the pulpit as his platform of pretense on Saturday and then he played his games of infidelity and immorality during the week. When Mary Lou shared pictures of Leroy and his mistress that she had found in the trunk of the car, she received shock from many who wanted to remain in total disbelief.

Regardless of her photos of clear evidence, Leroy *was not* removed from being a pastor. The Conference Committee voted to move Leroy on to Pensacola from Knoxville even though it was an absolutely "*well known fact*" *that* Leroy was boldly having an adulterous affair with that woman who had been so feared in the Knoxville SDA Church. Please read the articles from Ministry Magazine to review the standards that should be used for fallen pastors:

https://rb.gy/862dkw

https://rb.gy/p91qo0

King James Bible

For nothing is secret, that shall not be made manifest; neither anything hid, that shall not be known and come abroad. Luke 8:17

New Living Translation

For all that is secret will eventually be brought into the open, and everything that is concealed will be brought to light and made known to all. Luke 8:17

King James Version

If God be for you who then can be against you? Romans 8:31

CHAPTER 5 PART 7
Blessings Beyond Bondage

For every woman who now is married to an adulterous man who also happens to be a Pastor, please do not despair. My heart goes out to you as my prayers go up for you. Know that God's ever watchful eye is accounting for every truth that you have told that has been received as an untruth. You can also always be assured that God is also keeping track of every untruth that your adulterous husband has told which has been accepted as total truth.

You may be going through a time of *turbulent trouble,* that untruthfully places you as the one offending your husband in the sight of the congregation and "powers that be". While the real truth is not being revealed on your behalf and you watch those staunch supporters who have placed themselves as "pastor pleasers", accepting your husband's lies, regardless of their refusal to believe his immoral actions, in the very end, he will have to admit to the truth before everything is said and done.

It was my Mother who always said,

"What does not come out in the wash, will come out in the rinse."

She learned that regardless of who it is and who is supporting them in their lies, no matter what it is that they think they are getting away with, *God will bring the truth forth* in the end.

When Leroy Hemingway managed to get moved, by *the majority vote* from members of the South Central Conference Committee, from Knoxville to Pensacola, even after his adultery was proven (with actual pictures) by my Mother and reported by members of that church, the lies and adultery followed him straight to Pensacola, where he continued his affair once again with the same Knoxville woman. As the Senior Pastor, he eventually became involved with a new affair and Pensacola woman. It was in Pensacola that Mary Lou finally left Leroy without looking back.

When the truth came out in the Pensacola newspaper about how Leroy had violently struck his new girlfriend in the head, with a hammer so hard that her skull could be seen at the emergency room, members all over South Central Conference had additional confirmation about who the liar had been all along. That awful offense provided him with an orange jumpsuit and a personal jail cell. This also reminded the committee who had voted to support Pastor Hemingway, of their terrible decision to disregard the report that Mary Lou had brought to them before they decided to move Leroy from Knoxville to Pensacola.

All the lies and bogus stories that Leroy had projected as truth throughout Toledo and the 4 church districts of His assignments, now had come to their much needed impasse.

God's truth always wins in God's time.

Additional Information FelT several other blows. She observed the suspect holding a metal hammer. The suspect then dragged the victim back into the bedroom and attempted to place her into a closet. As she was screaming and begging the suspect to stop. The victim pleaded with the suspect to allow her to seek medical help. She told him that she would not call the Police if he would let her get help. The suspect then drove the victim to Baptist Hospital

R E T U R N

This Warrant was received by this department at
on the ____ day of ____ A.D. 19 ____ County, Florida,
and executed in ____ County,
Florida on the ____ day of ____
A.D. 19 ____ by arresting the within named

Arresting officer ____ Department

Date and time of service ____

Place of service ____

REMARKS

IN ____ COURT

CASE NO. ____ COUNTY

STATE OF FLORIDA
vs.

W A R R A N T
ORDER TO TAKE INTO CUSTODY
STATE OF FLORIDA

In the name of the State of Florida, to the Law Enforcement Officers of said County

WHEREAS, ____ has made on oath that on the ____ day
of ____ A.D. 19 ____ in the County
afore said one ____
did unlawfully violate ____

In the above named ____

This Warrant is a command to arrest instanter

Contrary to the law in such case and provided, and against the peace and dignity of the State of Florida.

____ and bring said person before the court to be dealt with according to law.

Given under my hand and seal this ____ day ____ A.D. 19 ____

(Seal)

Judge/Deputy Clerk

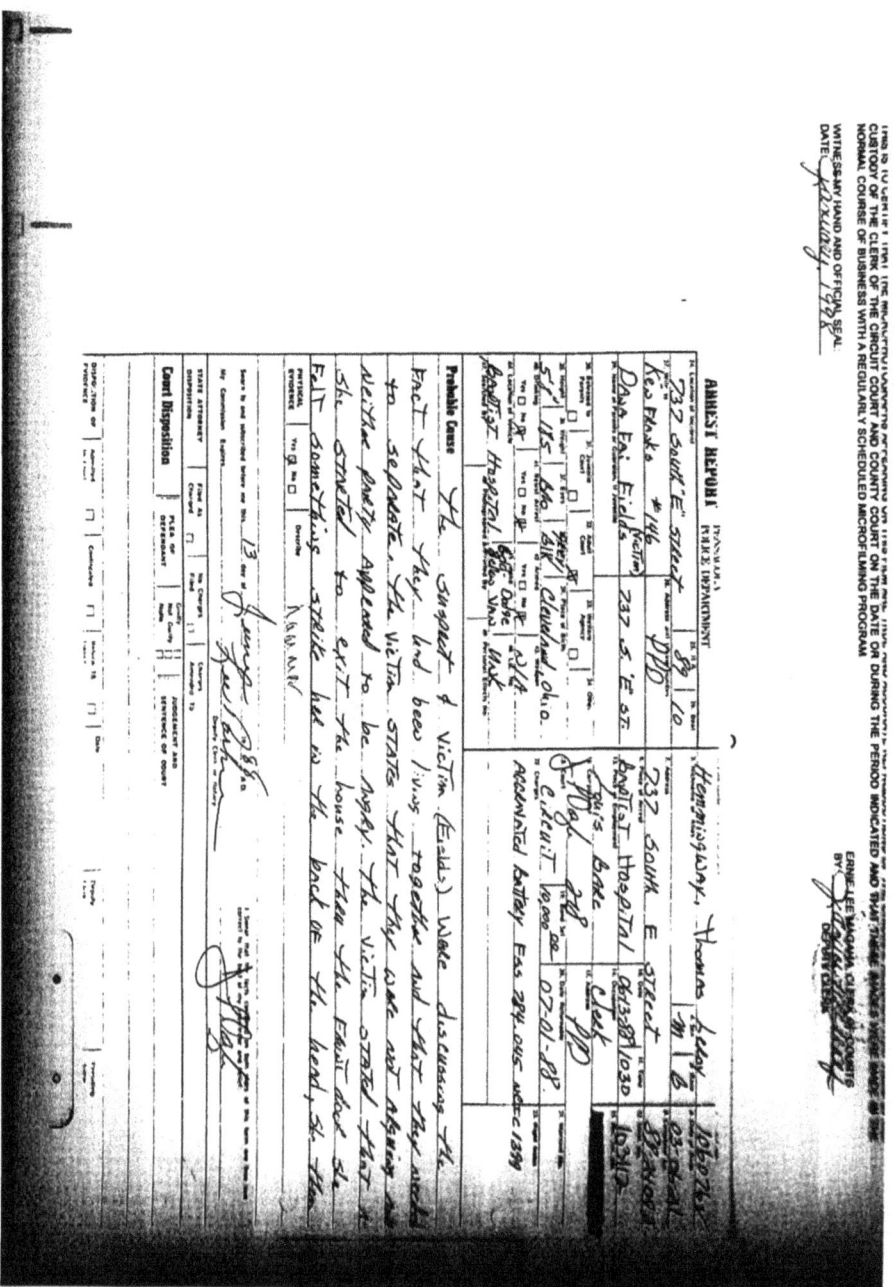

ARREST REPORT
(PANAMA)
POLICE DEPARTMENT

Probable Cause: The suspect & victim (Fields) were discussing the fact that they had been living together and that they wanted to separate. The victim states that they were not abusing each other party, appeared to be angry. The victim stated that she started to exit the house than the victim love she felt something strike her in the back of the head. She then

None

Court Disposition

178

Petway/13540   Judge Heflin/d 13917

ORDER WITHHOLDING ADJUDICATION OF GUILT
AND PLACING DEFENDANT ON PROBATION

STATE OF FLORIDA   In the ___Circuit___ Court

            Plaintiff

       VS   of ___Escambia___ County, Florida

THOMAS LEROY HEMMINGWAY

          Defendant   Case No. ___88-2634CFA___

This cause coming on this day to be heard before me, and you, the defendant, _____

___THOMAS LEROY HEMMINGWAY___, being now present before me, and you

having: ~~ENTERED A PLEA OF GUILTY TO~~
ENTERED A PLEA OF NOLO CONTENDERE TO
~~BEEN FOUND GUILTY BY THE VERDICT OF A JURY OF~~
~~BEEN FOUND GUILTY BY THE COURT TRYING THE CASE WITHOUT A JURY OF~~

the offense of ___Count 1: Aggravated Battery-Use of Deadly Weapon___

_____

_____

. appearing to the satisfaction of the Court; that you are not likely again to engage in a criminal course of conduct, and that the ends of justice and the welfare of society do not require that you should presently be adjudged guilty and suffer the penalty authorized by law;

Now, therefore, it is ordered and adjudged that the adjudication of guilt and imposition of sentence are hereby withheld, and that you are hereby placed on probation for a period of ___Two (2) years___ under the supervision of the Department of Corrections and its officers, such supervision to be subject to the provisions of the laws of this State.

It is further ordered that you shall comply with the following conditions of probation:

(1) Not later than the fifth day of each month, you will make a full and truthful report to your Probation Officer on the form provided for that purpose.
(2) You will pay to the State of Florida the amount of **Thirty Dollars ($30)** per month toward the cost of your supervision unless otherwise waived in compliance with Florida Statutes.
(3) You will not change your residence or employment or leave the county of your residence without first procuring the consent of your Probation Officer.
(4) You will neither possess, carry or own any weapons or firearm without first securing the consent of your Probation Officer.
(5) You will live and remain at liberty without violating any law. A conviction in a court of law shall not be necessary in order for such a violation to constitute a violation of your probation.
(6) You will not use intoxicants to excess; nor will you visit places where intoxicants, drugs or other dangerous substances are unlawfully sold, dispensed or used.
(7) You will work diligently at a lawful occupation and support any dependents to the best of your ability as directed by your Probation Officer.
(8) You will promptly and truthfully answer all inquiries directed to you by the Court or the Probation Officer, and allow the Officer to visit in your home, at your employment site or elsewhere, and you will comply with all instructions he may give you.
(9) Make restitution as determined by Probation and Parole.
(10) Pay $234.50 costs.

You are hereby placed on notice that the Court may at any time rescind or modify any of the conditions of your probation, or may extend the period of probation as authorized by law, or may discharge you from further supervision; and that if you violate any of the conditions of your probation, you may be arrested and the Court may revoke your probation, adjudge you guilty and impose any sentence which it might have imposed before placing you on probation.

It is further ordered that when you have reported to the Probation Officer and have been instructed as to the conditions of probation you shall be released from custody if you are in custody and if you are at liberty on bond, the sureties thereon shall stand discharged from liability.

It is further ordered that the Clerk of this Court file this order in his office, record the same in the Minutes of the Court, and forthwith provide certified copies of same to the Probation Officer for his use in compliance with the requirements of law.

DONE AND ORDERED IN OPEN COURT, this the ___27th___ day of ___July___ 19 _88_.

_____
Judge

I acknowledge receipt of a certified copy of this order and that the conditions have been explained to me.

Date: _____

                                 Probationer

Instructed by: _____

                                  Original: Cr
                                  Copies:

DC1-900B (8-86)

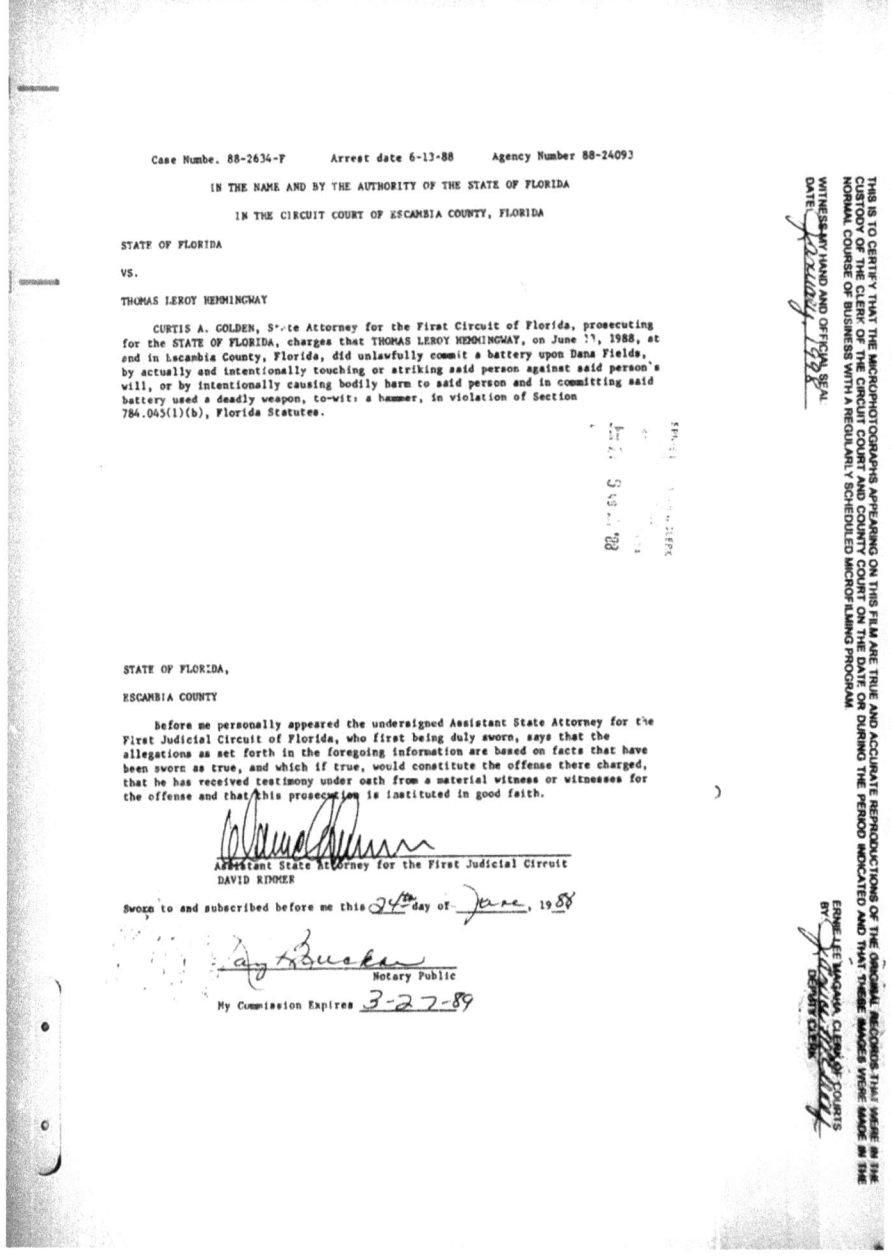

Case Numbe. 88-2634-F   Arrest date 6-13-88   Agency Number 88-24093

IN THE NAME AND BY THE AUTHORITY OF THE STATE OF FLORIDA

IN THE CIRCUIT COURT OF ESCAMBIA COUNTY, FLORIDA

STATE OF FLORIDA

VS.

THOMAS LEROY HEMMINGWAY

    CURTIS A. GOLDEN, S'·te Attorney for the First Circuit of Florida, prosecuting for the STATE OF FLORIDA, charges that THOMAS LEROY HEMMINGWAY, on June 1?, 1988, at and in Escambia County, Florida, did unlawfully commit a battery upon Dana Fields, by actually and intentionally touching or striking said person against said person's will, or by intentionally causing bodily harm to said person and in committing said battery used a deadly weapon, to-wit: a hammer, in violation of Section 784.045(1)(b), Florida Statutes.

STATE OF FLORIDA,

ESCAMBIA COUNTY

    before me personally appeared the undersigned Assistant State Attorney for the First Judicial Circuit of Florida, who first being duly sworn, says that the allegations as set forth in the foregoing information are based on facts that have been sworn as true, and which if true, would constitute the offense there charged, that he has received testimony under oath from a material witness or witnesses for the offense and that this prosecution is instituted in good faith.

Assistant State Attorney for the First Judicial Circuit
DAVID RIMMER

Sworn to and subscribed before me this 24th day of June, 1988

Notary Public

My Commission Expires 3-27-89

The Escambia Court Documents above are certified court copies of T. Leroy Hemingway's incidents in Pensacola, Florida during 1988.

Arrest date 6-13-88

Agency **Number** 88-24093

IN **THE NAME** AND BY **THE** AUTHORITY OF **THE STATE OF FLORIDA**

IN **THE** CIRCUIT **COURT OF** ESCAMBIA **COUNTY,** FLORIDA

Case Numbe: 88-2634-F

vs.

THOMAS **LEROY** HEMMINGWAY

CURTIS A. **GOLDEN, State** Attorney for the **First** Circuit of Florida, prosecuting for the **STATE OF FLORIDA,** charges that **THOMAS LEROY HEMMINGWAY,** on June 13, 1988, at and in Escambia County, Florida, did unlawfully commit a battery upon Dana Fields, by actually and intentionally touching or striking said person against said person's will, or by intentionally causing bodily harm to said person and in committing said battery used a deadly weapon, to-wit: a hammer, in violation of Section 784.045(1)(b), Florida Statutes. **STATE OF** FLORIDA

Jun 21 9 48 All '08

WITNESS MY **HAND AND OFFICIAL** SEAL: DATE:

January 199

ERNIEL PINS - MA, CLERK

NORMAL COURSE OF BUSINESS WITH A REGULARLY SCHEDULED MICROFILMING PROGRAM. CUSTODY OF THE CLERK OF THE CIRCUIT COURT AND COUNTY COURT ON THE DATE OR DURING THE PERIOD INDICATED AND THAT THESE IMAGES WERE MADE IN THE THIS IS TO CERTIFY THAT THE MICROPHOTOGRAPHS APPEARING ON THIS FILM ARE TRUE AND ACCURATE REPRODUCTIONS OF THE ORIGINAL RECORDS THAT WERE IN THE STATE OF FLORIDA,

ESCAMBIA COUNTY

Before me personally appeared the undersigned Assistant State Attorney for the First Judicial Circuit of Florida, who first being duly sworn, says that the allegations as set forth in the foregoing information are based on facts that have been sworn as true, and which if true, would constitute the offense there charged, that he has received testimony under oath from a material witness or witnesses for the offense and that this prosecution is instituted in good faith.

Assistant State Atorney for the First Judicial Circuit
DAVID RIMMER

Jur

e.

Sworn to and subscribed before me this
24 **day** of tire, 1958

I have included these documents to provide evidence of his psychological disorders for those who "would not" and also for those who "still do not" believe what he actually did and was capable of doing.

"Only God" kept Mary Lou throughout her marriage to Leroy especially when she returned to him in Pensacola. This incident as officially documented above, happened over a year after Mary Lou had left Pensacola and was divorced from Leroy Hemingway.

The final and ultimate blessing that came beyond all of the bondage from Leroy Hemingway's horrid acts, was that Mary Lou walked away *alive*, with the breath of life that God had given to her, still in her *right mind*, and with the brilliance to still use the many gifts that God had given to her. Mary Lou had definitely been truly blessed and miraculously spared beyond bondage.

Even though Mary Louise had passed away many years before, the hopes, dreams and prayers that she had for Mary Lou had covered Mary Lou's life. The prayers of a Godly Mother are a lifelong treasure to her children.

King James Bible

He shall cover thee with his feathers, and under his wings shalt thou trust: his truth shall be thy shield and buckler. Psalm 91:4

Weeping may endure for a night but joy cometh in the morning. Psalms 30:5

Behold, I will do a new thing; now it shall spring forth; shall ye not know it? I will even make a way in the wilderness, and rivers in the desert. Isaiah 43:19

CHAPTER 6 PART 1
Blessing Believers
Choosing Joy Despite Difficulties

Almost two years after our Father's death, our Mother married her childhood friend, Leroy Hemingway. While married to Leroy Hemingway, Mary Lou had the wonderful opportunity of becoming a pastor's wife. In the four church districts that she assisted Leroy in, Mary Lou found the journey of her second marriage easier because of the friendships that she made with so many of the members. Wherever Leroy was assigned, Mary Lou found favor with the parishioners. The natural love that Mary Lou had for others shone like the noontide sun.

Natchez, Mississippi was the very first district that Leroy was assigned to pastor in the summer of 1979. Leaving Toledo after 30 years was no problem for Mary Lou. She had experienced so many unbelievable challenges within those 30 years. Moving away from Toledo was like sweeping away the cobwebs that had lingered within the corners of her memory. Of course she would miss the cherished Toledo friends and also her family members that lived in Detroit and Cleveland. Yet, it was time for a change and her change had come with a huge move.

In Natchez, Mary Lou became the first lady of 3 church memberships. The largest church of the 3 was Triumphant Seventh-day Adventist Church. It is located in Natchez. Then there was another membership in Woodville that consisted of mainly two sisters who had prayer meeting services within the house trailer where one of them resided. On many of those prayer meetings, the most awesome southern dinner would be served to Leroy and Mary Lou before the prayer meeting began. I was blessed to have been a part of one of those prayer meetings while visiting my Mother during a holiday leave from Oakwood College. It was one of the best experiences of southern hospitality that I have ever been privileged to know.

The third Mississippi Membership of Leroy's pastoral assignment was in Fayette. The first Elder and his wife, Mr. and Mrs. Edwards, were also wonderfully kind to Leroy and Mary Lou. They also had plenty of southern hospitality to share with their pastor and first lady whenever services took place. It was in Fayette that I learned about "white spaghetti", a dish that does not include tomato sauce as an ingredient. The members of Fayette were also eager to benefit from the talent and guidance of their friendly pastoral leadership. They were also eager to show their "southern hospitality" to their Pastor and his wife.

Mary Lou and Leroy lived in a parsonage that was owned by the South Central Conference. It was a beautiful brick ranch style home with a fireplace in the family den and plenty of space to share for guests. It also had nice acreage and was not far from the Natchez Church. Mary Lou loved living in the parsonage. It was like the brick house that she had always wanted to purchase while married to Hugh.

Leroy loved to show off his culinary skills and Mary Lou did not mind him doing so at all. She had spent so many years within numerous kitchens helping Mary Louise prepare meals for wealthy families. Her years of being Hugh's wife and also her years of Motherhood had given her all the additional years of perfecting the title she called "head cook and chief bottle washer".Mary Lou was very content to let Leroy do most of the cooking.

Whenever there was a need, Mary Lou would play the piano or organ for services. She helped Leroy in any way that she could with his duties. Leroy could also play the piano and organ. His style of accompaniments was favored by many of the members who loved his gospel arrangements as well as his showmanship while playing them.

The Natchez, Woodville and Fayette members of Mississippi loved Mary Lou because she was loving to them. Mary Lou was easy to approach and showed sincere concern about the members that she served. Her ears were always keenly open to be attentive, while listening to the needs of those who had a problem to share. Her automatic suggestion to have prayer with those who had struggles brought additional comfort to the members who were in need of spiritual support.

There was a well-known understanding among some of the South Central Conference Workers that whenever someone was sent to Mississippi, they were being sent there because of some "lesson of retribution" that needed to be learned or because they had to "pay their initial dues" as being "the rookies" within the conference. Serving there was likened to some kind of unspoken "pastoral punishment" among some of the ministers and their wives. Despite that longtime legacy among the leaders, Mary Lou did not mind even by the least bit for serving within Mississippi. She was honored to serve the people *wherever* Leroy was assigned. Because of her mindset to bless the believers, she received reciprocal blessings from the members that she was serving.

Around 1981, when Leroy was given the assignment to pastor the Adventist Congregation in Bessemer, Alabama. Mary Lou once again rose to the occasion to bless the members. Leroy's assignment within the Bessemer District included the memberships of Adamsville and Leeds.

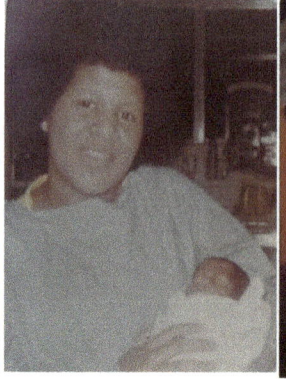

Marla with children in Bessemer briefly, during Mary Lou and Leroy's pastorate there. The center picture shows Marla in Toledo with her first born, Ronald Jr. Miya and Marla (Lala) are shown in the last picture. Miya's standing behind Lala. Mary Lou is in photo #1.

As favored as Mary Lou had been in Mississippi, she also found favor from the members in Alabama. There she became so attached to some of the members that they started calling her "Mom Hemingway". Those bonds of maternal influence remained in place not only while Leroy was pastoring in Alabama, but until the very last days of Mary Lou's life.

Even now, seven years after her death, she is still referred to as "Mom Hemingway" and "Mama" by those who chose to accept her as "an adopted mother" while she was serving as their first lady. Because of the love that they received from her influential guidance and leadership, Mary Lou was readily accepted and included within the homes and within the hearts of the Alabama members.

Mary Lou loved living in Bessemer because she had always been one to frequent thrift stores. In fact, she had also been known to introduce and teach some of her parishioners about "the blessing of thrifting.This was a skill that she had perfected and shared with her close friends for 30 years while residing in Toledo. Essie Darnell who was one of Mary Lou's best friends, testified even within the last breaths of her life, to the fun filled memories that she and Mary Lou encountered while finding treasures during their rummage sale and thrift store adventures.

The Birmingham and surrounding areas had some of the best "bargain barns" that any thrifter could ever hope for. Years later when I became a teacher in Birmingham, Mary Lou would spend many days revisiting "her places" as she affectionately called her favorite thrift stores. She would have the time of her life thrifting, while I was teaching. By the time 3:30 came around, she would be happily waiting for me in the school parking lot, eager to give and show me her "thrift praise report" for all of the beautiful bargains that she had been blessed with for that day.

The blessings that Mary Lou shared with the believers in Alabama are too numerous to tell in one chapter. The lives that she embraced by the encouragement that she gave was monumentally affirmative for those who respected her influence. Mary Lou was never selfish about lending a helping hand to anyone in need. She remembered the helping hands of Mary Louise and she lived out the legacy that had been lived right in front of her as she developed into womanhood. Sharing that legacy with those she served was as natural as breathing air, because it was at the core of her character.

When the conference committee voted for Leroy to be assigned to the Knoxville, Tennessee District, in 1983, Mary Lou was somewhat reluctant. There had been rumors about a female member who had mothered an illegitimate child for one of the former pastors who had been assigned there several years before Leroy's assignment. According to the gossip around the "Adventist Grapevine" at that time, there were detailed reports about how this woman was notorious for her adulterous attitude and activities. This was "the talk of the town" among Adventists not only within the Knoxville Communities but also within other Adventist Circles nationwide.

Because of this known fact, the conference committee members were careful to send "seasoned men" to pastor this district. They did not want any more scandal attached to the Knoxville Membership within that District. It was a very sad day when Leroy fell prey to the adulterous snares of the woman who he chose to break his ministerial vows and marriage vows with. His decision would eventually cost him not only the wife that he had always coveted and initially desired, but also the Adventist Ministry which he had also yearned for as well.

When I visited my Mother in Knoxville, Tennessee, I found her to be as committed to her members as she had always been in the previous church districts where she had served as a pastor's wife. Mary Lou was always well loved and supported by most of the members wherever Leroy was pastor. She had no different favor in the Knoxville and Harriman Churches that comprised the Knoxville Church District. The Knoxville Members were very fond of their lovely "Sister Hemingway".

I was ever so happy to see not only the love but more so the loyalty that some of the members had formed between themselves and my Mother. I never ever trusted Leroy Hemingway. He had proven, even before leaving Toledo, the viperous ways that he operated with.

When I flew from New York City to Knoxville for one Thanksgiving Holiday, Leroy was sure to be on his best behavior. He always wanted his peers and parishioners to believe that he welcomed me as if I were his own blood daughter. That was the way that he consistently camouflaged his devilish darkness. But what he never fully understood was how intimately God was watching over every second of his life. If Leroy had ever known the unlimited amount of silent personal petitions that I faithfully sent to God on behalf of my Mother's life, he would have feared to enter into the foolishness that led him to his own misfortunes and spiral downfall.

As Leroy's pastoral assignment unfolded, so did his adulterous affair. He and his mistress became so engaged in their escapades that church members learned of their relationship. Mary Lou suffered in silent sorrow, week after week, and month after month. Her complaints to those with administrative power over Leroy were seemingly ignored.

He was telling his superiors that Mary Lou was going through "The Change". (menopause) Leroy successfully led his supervisors to believe that Mary Lou's hormonally imbalanced imagination was responsible for the reports that she was sharing with them. For quite a while, that was the belief across the conference for those who chose to accept Leroy's lies. Unfortunately, that kind of improper decision making is often the case when ministers are involved in adultery.

There is often a cycle of "administrative denial" to dismiss what the pastor's wives are reporting in defense of the pastor and his reputation. Some Pastors usually cover their fellow pastors as an act of loyalty. Like an unbreakable brotherhood, this bonding often covers a multitude of sinful acts, especially, when adultery is involved.

Why are the pastor's wives and even the parishioners so frequently overlooked and ignored when reporting factual issues of adultery involving their husbands and pastors? While they are seeking out help for their spouses and spiritual leaders, why should their reports be dismissed as rumors, imaginations and troublemaking? What could happen if Immediate interventions were given in response to any issues of not only adultery, but any inappropriate acts of offensiveness? **Pastors are not immune to being human and in need of intervention.**

Mary Lou stands as a South Central Conference First Lady with her second husband, Pastor Thomas Leroy Hemingway. She was faithful to him although he was unfaithful.

Were it not for one of the faithful church members, Mrs. Ada Jones, (who I shall call a "sisterly saint") taking Mary Lou under her motherly wings, who knows how Mary Lou's Mindset would have survived this scornful period of her life. **"Mother Jones", as she was faithfully called by those in Knoxville, made herself "a committee of one" to stand by Mary Lou at this time.**

There were also others who also stood by their beloved "Sister Hemingway" because they knew what was really going on between Leroy and his mistress. Terry and Michael Harris were very supportive of Mother throughout her time as their First Lady. Terry's Mother, Mrs. Lucille Hill, had been one of Mary Lou's dearest college friends at Oakwood. **Mike and Terry did anything that they could to show their concern for Mary Lou.** When Mother Jones decided to become an earthly angel of mercy to Mary Lou, she did everything that she could to stand behind her pastor's wife. Ada Jones became a fearless friend to Mary Lou because she knew that my Mother was being mistreated. She was the Godly Warrior who drove Mary Lou to the bus station when my Mother decided to come and stay with me in Rochester, New York, where I was teaching at the time.

When Hubert, (who was also living in Rochester) and I picked our Mother up at the Greyhound Station in Rochester, she looked like she had been in the battle of her life. She had lost weight and more than anything, her countenance that had always been vibrantly bright, was darkened by discouragement and depression due to *Leroy's bold affair.* It was a startling and shamefully shocking moment to see our Mother without her naturally appealing joy. It made me think about the day that I had been praying and heard the Lord tell me,

"You need to keep on praying for your Mother because she is living with a demon."

As soon as I got off my knees, I quickly called my Mother and told her what I heard the Lord tell me. Then I told her to get out of Knoxville and come to live with me in Rochester. I was relieved when she finally got away from Knoxville heading to New York. Yet when she stepped off that Greyhound Bus, I was angered *beyond outrage* to immediately see the emotional impact that Leroy's evil had taken upon our Mother. I never told either Hubert or my Mother how fully incensed I felt on that day. Only the love and concern that I had for my Mother and the strength of the Holy Spirit's biddings, constrained my soul on that particular day.

Even though Mary Lou was in the midst of a tumultuous journey that was satanically meant to destroy her peace, love and stability, our Mother's beautiful smile still shone as she faced Hubert, her firstborn and Michelle, her last born, "bonus baby". She had the peaceful serenity of knowing that there was genuine supportiveness, safety and strength encompassing her while finally within the boundaries of her very own adult children. Despite the demonic bondage that surrounded her in Knoxville, she was now surrounded with the loving bond that she needed from her own flesh and blood. In spite of her difficulties, *our Mother chose joy* because it was the greater choice that she relied upon to find the inner peace that God wanted her to have.

The group class photo is from the 1985-86 school year at Rochester Junior Academy. Mary Lou's granddaughter and first grandchild was in this class. (3rd student to the far right.) Mary Lou spent part of the school year in Rochester during this school year. She was well loved by my students and Danielle was happy to have her "Nana" close by.

In the right photo, Danielle is the third girl. (left to right) Her mother, Evelyn, made that pilgrim's outfit for Danielle and for her classroom Thanksgiving Celebration. This was the only time that my Mother was ever able to help out in my classroom and also the only time that I taught any one in my family. Danielle was a brilliant student academically.

Michelle Duncan is first girl and Lorna Garcia is in the center. Both are current educators.

King James Bible

Be not deceived; God is not mocked: for whatsoever a man soweth, that shall he also reap. Galatians 6:7

King James Bible

And we know that all things work together for good to them that love God, to them who are the called according to his purpose. Romans 8:31

CHAPTER 6 PART 2

Blessing Believers

"Experiencing Marital Infidelity While Sojourning Through Dark Days, Depression and Divorce"

During the months that Mary Lou spent in Rochester, she continued to bless believers that she came in contact with. She was a blessing to my students whenever she volunteered in my classroom. Her help was more than a blessing to some of them, because she often talked me out of giving them punishments that they deserved beyond any shadow of doubt. All of my students loved Mrs. Hemingway because they felt comfortable around her and they also saw that she was easy to love.

In addition, Mary Lou spent requested weeks with two of a recently widowed father's children while he was out of town fulfilling job duties. Because the father's job took him all over the country, Mary Lou instantly became an added blessing to that family who had recently experienced the loss of the wonderful matriarch within their household. The children trusted her unassuming, yet caring and respectable approach to supervising them because they were at pre-teen and teenage stages within their lives. They were dealing with enough just trying to cope with the loss of their beloved mother. Mary Lou brought no added stress to them when she spent time in their home.

One of the greatest ways that Mary Lou blessed others was in the way that she left her words of encouragement with others. Though in the midst of her own trials and tribulations, she did not shrink in spirit to share a positive word whenever she could. Of greatest significance was her ability to have been able to spend time with her young grandchildren. Hubert's children were blessed to have had those precious months with their "Nana" as she had all of her grandchildren call her. That was a special time for them but equally for her because that was the longest time that she had ever spent in their home town.

In the early months of 1986, Mary Lou received a call from Leroy's supervisor. He encouraged Mary Lou to return to Leroy because the conference committee had voted to move him out of Knoxville to Pensacola, Florida. Why the majority of the committee would entertain that kind of a thought seemed ludicrous to me. Inviting our Mother to be involved in anything even connected to Leroy outraged my spirit. Especially when they knew that Leroy was being intentionally adulterous.

"What in Heaven's name were these men of responsibility thinking? How could they even feel good about themselves let alone this decision that directly impacted the lives of innocent members and most of all the innocent marital choices of Mary Lou?"

Our Mother had not been the one having an adulterous affair that the whole Knoxville Church District knew about. She had not been the one who had purposefully disregarded her marital vows before God and all of Heaven. Yet, Mary Lou was the one that was being asked to overlook all of the adulterous scorn, deceit and lies that were being directed at her.

The conference committee was asking far too much of a woman who had already taken way too much. Mary Lou had taken much more than any man or woman on that conference committee would have ever taken from their own spouses if they had been in her same situation. How *hypocritically insensitive* for any of them to set those kinds of expectations for anyone.

The fact that they not only set them for our Mother and also had encouraged her to accept them was beyond absolute reproach. They would have **never** wanted their own Mothers to be presented with such absolutely asinine standards.

It more than outraged me to think that "men of the cloth" could create such a hellish deal. *In my estimation, they were asking our Mother not only to return to the devil, but also to dance with the devil at his celebration party of relocation in Pensacola.* That's what made the whole situation ludicrously lame as far as I was concerned.

One may say that the committee was only trying to show compassion and forgiveness to Leroy by giving him a second chance. Yet this kind of *"second chance mentality"* often places the wives of adulterous pastors in more jeopardy, scorn and havoc than words can ever describe. What these first ladies endure in order to help their adulterous husbands save and restore their ministries is truly unfortunate and unbelievably shocking.

Not only within the SDA Denomination but in **all** denominations, this kind of "second chance mentality" occurs to cover adulterous ministers. It is noble to forgive but there needs to be some real truth about restoration for the wives of these ministers who have been given brokenness to their marriages. **Those who are sitting in seats of supervision need to take *deeper contemplation* about how they can provide intervention for the women who they are expecting to forgive such erring husbands.**

These *wounded women* are also in need of active consideration and immediate help while still walking in ministry beside these anointed men of God who have disregarded their marital vows. Where there is mercy and grace for the *"men of the cloth"*, there should also be mercy and grace to empathize and help the needs of the first ladies who are so often "suffering in silence". Finally, there needs to be some professional therapy mandated as well as marital counseling before *any* steps are made for reassignment of pastors involved in adultery. In order for true healing to take place, true interventions need to transpire for marital teams that are struggling and that have struggled with the storms of infidelity.

Furthermore, why is rebaptism usually not part of the restoration equation when adultery has been a part of a minister's intentional waywardness? Isn't the Word of God and church standards applicable to all of us who err? Why do some adulterous pastors lose their credentials, while other adulterous pastors are allowed to keep their credentials without any consequences?

Romans 3:23 says, "For all have sinned and come short of the glory of God." Often ministers' sins of adultery are frequently "swept under the rug" and covered up as those adulterous pastors are moved out of town and on to new congregations.

Does this pattern of permissiveness find favor with God's Word?

Whenever I contemplate the experiences that my Mother went through during this period of marriage to Leroy, I know that "*only God*", could have brought her through so much dissension, depression and drama. To have been *shunned* and gossiped about by individuals who had known her for many decades was beyond deceitful. Then for Mary Lou to have had similar betrayals from family members was also even more than deceitful.

It has often been quoted that,

"Blood is thicker than water."

If that was the case, why were some family members adding fuel to the proverbial fire, especially when they were being told directly by Mary Lou herself, exactly what was really happening with her treacherous husband, Leroy? What I witnessed first-hand during this timeframe was how individuals will deviate from truth when it makes them uncomfortable and uncertain, especially when they want to remain *uninvolved.* One really gets to see who the *"real folks"* are when tough times of challenge press down and when questions surround the character of a person.

It is in times like these that one also learns their true status from those who have called themselves friends and family.

In this time when Mary Lou needed the most love and support from all of those who had been within her arena of comradery, she could not find dependability in *some*. It seemed sometimes that the weight of the world was upon my Mother's back as she watched the scenarios within her world unfold.

One of the greatest lessons that I ever learned from my Mother's example at this time was how to walk boldly in the face of gossipers and backbiters while ignoring their lies, slander and gossip. By watching her first hand, I learned how to go through life's storms without letting the wind, rain, thunder and lightning of life's storms damage me. If Mother had not been linked to the Lord because of Mary Louise's example, I don't think that she could have survived this period of her life with her entire sanity intact. Mary Louise had withstood the storm from Wright Battle. Mary Lou witnessed how Mary Louise kept her faith throughout that difficult time of trouble and deceit.

To this day, I have no acceptable reasons as to why faithful women are often the scorned targets of their husbands' adulterous affairs. It is as though some folk thrive on excusing a man's indiscretions because of some negativity that they think his wife has caused. How often that is just not the case. Why this mentality still prevails within so many warped minds is still troubling to me.

There wasn't anything pleasant about that period of time within Mary Lou's life. She was bearing a cross that was far too heavy, especially after all that had already transpired within her life. Watching her manage the scandal, shunning and shame surrounding her, was tremendously difficult and dark. It at times seemed as though this experience was like a winding staircase without end.

I had to do a tremendous amount of praying after my Mother said she would return back to be by Leroy's side. How I ever tried to get her to change her mind before she left Rochester and got on the plane. As dreary as the Rochester weather was that day, the climate of my mood was even more dreary. *Mary Lou's Mindset* was beyond changing. She had decided to give her marriage a second chance.

For the members in Pensacola, my Mother's forgiveness to Leroy was their gain. They also benefited from the blessings of Mary Lou's Mindset while she was their First Lady. Mary Lou's forgiveness to Leroy could have been one of his greatest blessings and a true turning point within his life *"if"* he had allowed it to benefit him in that way. However, with Leroy's new assignment came his same old slick behavioral choices.

Those who had never known him before observed his patterns to be cold and insensitive toward their first lady. One of the Pensacola members, Brother Fenner, shared this story with me a few years back. In his own words he said,

"My wife always loved Sister Hemingway. When she noticed that the pastor was doing suspicious things and leaving Sister Hemingway alone, then we got more involved in checking up on Sister Hemingway. One particular time, my wife had called Sister Hemingway repeatedly using their residential number. Her call went to the same message that was recorded on our church's answering machine. I knew then that the pastor was forwarding their home phone calls to the church. Immediately my wife and I went to see Sister Hemingway. My wife knocked and knocked but there was no response. We decided to leave. But, as I was pulling out of their driveway, my wife said, **"Wait, I saw the curtains moving."** *So I drove back into the driveway and I went to the door and said,* **"Sister Hemingway, we know you are in there. Please open the door."**

Mary Lou did open the door and let those two members come inside. She was given the support and love from Mr. and Mrs. Fenner as if they were her very own blood brother and sister. Mary Lou then confirmed to them their suspicions about Leroy's indiscretions. He had not only continued to keep his relationship with his mistress from Knoxville, but also started new extra marital activities with new women.

If Mary Lou had not been the kind of person who had been a blessing to the believers within the churches that she served, she most likely would not have had the immediate support that she greatly needed in her time of greatest distress. Again, she had found much needed support right within the circle of her very own congregation. It was members like those and also her cousin Thelma Scott's daughter, Debbie Williams, who aided her to make her final exit from

Leroy's life. Jewel (Sams) Prigg was the *"Angel of Exit"* that drove Mary Lou to Huntsville, Alabama when she finally moved all of her personal belongings away from Pensacola.

Before moving to Huntsville, Mother came to live with me in Tennessee, where I was in Graduate School working on my Master's Degree in Counseling. During those months in Tennessee, Mary Lou spent many days in silent retrospect working through her feelings of disgust, sorrow, anger and remorse. She experienced many days of despondency. For the most part, I tried not to interfere with the process that Mother was going through. I knew that she needed that time to chisel through the layers of psychological torture that Leroy had shown her.

In so many ways it was good for Mary Lou to be away from all of her regular associates and family members. While within the stages of this healing process, she had the opportunity to be free from all the gossiping voices, naysayers and nosey spectators who had nothing positive to give her. Within the privacy of her own timetable, Mary Lou found her own way to dig deeply within the wells of her own personal worth. It was within those inner chambers that she remembered all that Mary Louise had shown her about trusting in the Lord.

That personal solitude and communion with God restored my Mother for the days that were ahead of her. While observing her during this healing process, I learned once again, just how resilient she could be. Though healing and deeply wounded from within, Mary Lou had not lost all of her luster. Behind all those layers of psychological abuse were still original layers of beauty, dignity, grace and God given strength.

I will never forget the day that I accompanied Mother to select a divorce attorney. She had taken the yellow pages and done a little research before narrowing her choice down to two men. When we went to the first lawyer, I could tell that he was not going to make the cut for being chosen. Although professional, that man was without genuine compassion. He was also showing a sign of racial indifference as well, because he appeared uncomfortable that we were black folk.

Moving on to the next attorney was where Mary Lou found her answers. That gentleman was a Christian. He had a Bible boldly sitting on the front of his desk where everyone could see. Without any fanfare within his presentation or reluctance toward interacting with Mother, the second attorney shared an approach that met the needs for her divorce process.

By the time she had gone through the months of waiting for the legal process to take its course, Mary Lou had found new courage and hope. She saw God use her attorney to miraculously work through several "legal loopholes" which saved her from any unnecessary difficulties and undue stress. In addition, Mary Lou was able to financially meet the cost for her divorce without paying exorbitant attorney fees.

When Spring rolled around, I sat at the back of the courtroom and watched my Mother become legally free from Leroy Hemingway. On that day, I saw total joy and reformation within her exuberant spirit. Shadows were lifted and burdens disappeared when the Judge spoke the words of liberation granting Mother's divorce. I had not seen that kind of relief on her face in years, as I heard her confidently say,

"Thank you Lord."

I knew that she was at peace and ready to move forward into the newness that God had waiting for her. It was one of the happiest moments that I had ever shared with her because I truly saw how liberated she felt on that glorious beginning of her new freedom.

Even after Mary Lou stopped being a pastor's wife, she still had the lifetime respect from her former members within all 4 states. Throughout the years that they came in contact with her through camp meetings, alumni, funerals, weddings or other special services at Oakwood, they always honored Mary Lou's presence with hugs and kisses to show their ongoing love and respect for her. Some of them even shared their own testimonies about how glad they were to see her independently doing fine.

In 1987 after Mary Lou had received her divorce from Leroy, she was given the opportunity of serving at Oakwood College as the Residence Dean at Carter Hall. I can still vividly remember the day that the Dean of Women, Mrs. Rita Jones met her in Peterson Hall on Oakwood's Campus. It was a bright sunny afternoon and Dean Jones seemed to have a very intensive look as she made her overview and initial observations. She ended the conversation with a prayer before the brief meeting ended. A couple of weeks later, Mary Lou was hired.

I was told by a member of the South Central Conference Committee, that the President of the South Central Conference, Elder Charles Dudley had mainly been responsible for speaking on Mary Lou's behalf concerning this assignment as a Residence Dean at Carter Hall. He felt that something needed to be done on Mary Lou's behalf because of the things that she had suffered during Leroy Hemingway's downward pastoral path.

Elder Dudley and his wonderful wife Etta (Maycock) Dudley had been classmates and dear friends with Mary Lou during 1945 through 1947. In fact, Etta and Mary Lou had been dormitory roommates during that same period of time of their collegiate classes and experiences. In the case of him being a man of great power and influence as well as a faithful friend to Mary Lou since 1945, President Charles Dudley used the status that God had blessed him with, to bless Mary Lou with the position she received to become a Dean at Oakwood. I don't think she would have received that job as a Residence and Girl's Dormitory Dean had Dr. Charles Dudley not spoken on her behalf.

What Charles Dudley did in that one meeting set the trajectory for Mary Lou's life for the remainder of her years. As he watched her blossom and rebound back into the vibrancy that she had shown as an Oakwood student from 1945 - 1947, Elder Charles Dudley gave Mary Lou a new name. He told her his name for her was being changed to "Mary New", because she had transformed into a vibrancy with new joy as she gained her new status as a Resident Dean at Oakwood's Carter Hall.

From that time forward, whenever "Uncle Charles" as my siblings and I called him came around our mother, he would reveal his larger than life smile and say, "MARY NEW" as he chuckled with joy. Whenever he and his awesome wife, Etta Maycock Dudley (Aunt Etta) invited our mother to spend time to visit within their home, those days of reuniting were like an Oakwood Reunion when Etta and Mary Lou were roommates. The Dudleys were two of Mary Lou's most dearest and loyal friends from 1945 until her death in 2013.

Their daughter Bonita Dudley Scott-Parker, who is the Owner, Proprietor and Fashion Designer at Sew Savoir-faire in Nashville, Tennessee, escorted her Mother to our Mother's Celebration of Life Memorial Service. She also created and made her Mother the most stunning royal blue dress for the service. Her father, Elder Charles Dudley had passed prior to Mary Lou in 2010.

ABOUT THE AUTHOR

Dr. Charles Edward Dudley, Sr., pastors the First Seventh-day Adventist Church of Shelbyville, Tennessee. For more than fifty-three years he has served the denomination as a pastor, administrator, teacher, humanitarian, church organizer, builder, historian, promoter, researcher, writer, innovator and world traveler. His interest is totally committed to the service of mankind in all parts of the world. He has a deep interest in people on all continents around the globe and constantly works to help build Christian relationships between every nation, kindred tongue and people.

He has served as an administrator for the Seventh-day Adventist denomination for more than thirty-one and half years. His book, They Who Hurt Brought Us, has sparked a deeper interest in African-American history worldwide. This book on the Genealogy of Ellen Gould Harmon White will challenge the reader.

THE GENEALOGY OF ELLEN GOULD HARMON WHITE

THE PROPHETESS OF THE SEVENTH-DAY ADVENTIST CHURCH, AND THE STORY OF THE GROWTH AND DEVELOPMENT OF THE SEVENTH-DAY ADVENTIST DENOMINATION AS IT RELATES TO AFRICAN-AMERICANS

CHARLES EDWARD DUDLEY, SR.

Dr. Charles Edward Dudley was truly a Man of God. He lived his entire career in the joy of serving God and God's People. I know of no other individual who sacrificed or surpassed his "*31 year*" record as a President at the SDA Conference Level. His dedication to his predominantly African American Members in the South Central Conference was truly timely and spiritually stellar. Within turbulent times of great danger, as a Seventh-day Adventist Administrator, Dr. Dudley fearlessly led 5 southern states, **Kentucky, Tennessee, Alabama, Mississippi, and Northern Florida** during the Civil Rights Era and far beyond.

The contributions he made, with his supportive, loyal and loving wife Etta, will never be forgotten nor will they ever be equaled. *Truly he was a man like the men who Ellen White refers to in her book, Education, page 100, Dr. Dudley would not be bought or sold.*

https://www.goodreads.com/quotes/7868146-the-greatest-want-of-the-world-is-the-want-o

ESDA | Dudley, Charles Edward, Sr. (1927–2010)

https://encyclopedia.adventist.org/article?id=7CEK

See page 264 for additional information about Dr. Dudley.

One of Elder Dudley's favorite hymns was: "Don't Take Your Eyes Off the Savior"

https://youtu.be/t15Emlxygt8?si=y81cOMkJzq6S-uic

President Charles E. Dudley and First Lady Etta Dudley were a dynamic duo for God.

Photo credit: This is a copy of the photo from Bonita (Dudley) Scott-Parker's profound documentation of her father's life in the memorial program that she designed, entitled, "Jesus Led Me All the Way."

Dr. Charles Edward Dudley, Sr.

February 1, 1927 – April 18, 2010

Tribute to a Legend
Sunday, April 25, 2010
12:00 noon

"Jesus Led Me All The Way"

Riverside Chapel Seventh-day Adventist Church
800 Youngs Lane – Nashville, Tennessee 37207
Pastor Furman F. Fordham II, Officiant
Dr. Charles E. Bradford, Eulogist

Etta and Mary Lou are posing in this photo at an Oakwood Alumni Weekend. I took this photo of "Aunt Etta" and my Mother after church at The Von Braun Civic Center during an Oakwood Alumni Weekend.

Etta (Maycock) Dudley and Mary Lou {Battle) Hemingway are at the old drinking fountain during their days as students back in 1945-1947. Etta is on the left side of the fountain in the plaid suit. Mary Lou is on the right side of the fountain in the red sweater and gray skirt. Photo credit: Mary Lou's Oakwood Photos

Mary Lou and Etta in June of 1947, on their Oakwood College Graduation Day. They remained faithful friends while still calling each other "roommate" from 1945 until Mary Lou's death in 2013. Photo Credit: Mary Lou's Oakwood Photos

In this Oakwood University Alumni Class Picture, the Class of 1947 are celebrating "40 years" since their college graduation. Mary Lou and Etta are seated front and center holding the "Class of '47" Banner. Mary Lou is wearing the black hat and yellow dress on the left and Etta is wearing the white dress on the right.

Pictured in the back row is Etta's husband and South Central Conference President, Elder Charles E. Dudley. *(See page 264 for additional information about Dr. C.E. Dudley.) He is standing first, on the back row of the left side.

Directly next to Elder Dudley is Elder Charles Bradford, who was a retired President of the North American Division of the Seventh-day Adventist Church. For more information about Dr. Bradford, see the links that follow:
https://youtu.be/oNB-qXaihX0?si=IiA1zxjWIo87Z_Wo   https://rb.gy/l6qufh

https://www.youtube.com/watch?v=fSfUOMjjkrw

Oh the joy that Mary Louise would have had if she had been alive to see the daughter that she raised working as a Residence Dean on the grounds of Oakwood University. Mary Louise would have been thrilled to have actually seen the prayers of her hopes fulfilled for the desired daughter of her heart. For Mary Lou, life had gone full circle. She was returning to the place where she had studied and graduated forty years earlier. Even more, Mary Lou was returning to the very grounds where Mary Louise had been a student and where Mary Louise had in fact even met Ellen G. White, one of the leaders responsible for Oakwood's Origins and also the most prolific and inspirational author of the Worldwide Seventh-day Adventist Church.

Mary Lou standing on the Oakwood University Campus as the Residence Dean at Carter Hall. She is happily wearing the Oakwood University Colors, blue and gold.

It was a very special time in Mary Lou's life. As she served the young ladies that were assigned to her dormitory, she gave serious guidance of encouragement, direction and at times correction. Her heart of love and loyalty for her alma mater was always evidenced by the unselfish, stellar service that she faithfully shared. Mary Lou had always loved Oakwood. She had *precious memories* that she had always maintained with her Oakwood friends and alumni. Now being a part of Oakwood's tradition through becoming a part of the faculty and staff meant more to Mary Lou than this world will ever know.

Mary Lou is sitting at the Oakwood University Church during an Alumni Weekend Service. She was dressed for Sabbath Services and adorned with her vibrant, sunshine smile.

As Mary Lou engaged in the business of mentoring young women, she led by example and shared some of her own personal triumphs. Nothing was ever too hard to accomplish as a Dean because Mary Lou's Mindset went with her to Oakwood. She took her life of faith and prayer back to the grounds that she had known at 20 years of age.

Being 62 years old meant nothing to Mary Lou. There were times when she put on her roller skates and was seen *"rolling with the students"* at the Oakwood Skating Rink. She said they were always amazed to see her agility and ease while they skated past her waving and saying,

"Hi Dean Hemingway!"

For Mary Lou, Oakwood was the best therapy that could have ever been given to a woman who had been through so much hardship. She was good for the Oakwood students and the Oakwood students were good for her. They took her mind away from all the bondage that she had known and gave her a new focus for the golden years of her personal story.

When it came to loving people, Mary Lou was a natural. She loved to talk and meet new people. When someone had a need to find a listening ear that was genuinely concerned, one could always be embraced by the empathic ears of Mary Lou.

Her discerning nature, blended with her willingness to care, brought a comfortable level of security to those who sought her out for encouragement. **There was nothing fake about Mary Lou.** Her genuine spirit transcended the spirit of those who were phony and everyone knew that "Dean Hemingway" was definitely "for real".

When one former graduate of Oakwood met me and found out that my Mother had served as an Oakwood Residence Dean in Carter Hall, immediately he questioned,

"Who is your Mother?"

When I replied, Dean Hemingway, then with great excitement, he immediately said,

*"**Dean Hemingway is your Mother? Oh, everybody knew that Dean Hemingway did not play when I was attending Oakwood. Dean Hemingway had a reputation for taking care of business. She was nice, but she did not play.**"*

I laughed with that former student because I knew exactly what he meant because it was my Mother who handled the discipline during my childhood. She was a firm and consistent disciplinarian that definitely did not play. So, I knew that the young man was telling the absolute truth.

Dr. Emerson Cooper, Retired Oakwood Chemistry Department Chairman and Mary Lou at a farewell dinner before she moved to California with me in 2007.

***Dr. Cooper was one of Mary Lou's Oakwood Classmates. Dr. Cooper was a man of brilliance and excellence. He left an iconic legacy at Oakwood.** https://www.youtube.com/watch?v=pB9yZD1pHIM*

Mary Lou loved being reunited with friends during every Oakwood Alumni Weekend. Here she is standing by Elder Lee Pascal who was the Oakwood Alumni Association President for many years. Seated next to him is Mrs. Edna Lett-Williamson who was a dear friend and classmate of Mary Lou. Mary Lou assisted the Oakwood Alumni Team throughout the 20 years that she served as a Dean. She annually volunteered at Blake Center helping register the alumni and preparing the alumni packets for distribution.

In addition to having the benefit of connecting with a younger generation, Mary Lou also had the opportunity to reconnect with former Oakwood Classmates who had retired and relocated from other areas of the country to the Huntsville Community. Because of her love of people, Mary Lou was happy to see her friends move to Huntsville. Most of them joined her as members of the University Church, which afforded Mary Lou the opportunity of having weekly fellowship with cherished friends as she had done before during her collegiate years.

Often, when I was visiting Mother, I had the privilege of seeing her interact with her old classmates after church services. It was like a mini alumni weekend every Sabbath as those seniors discussed various upcoming events, denominational news and other personal matters of interest regarding their adult children and grandchildren. Sometimes I felt totally invisible to this "close knit" group who had formed special bonds of friendship over four decades ago.

I was happy to see our Mother's life at a peaceful plateau. She certainly deserved to enjoy everything that her new assignment surrounded her with. This second journey that brought her back to live on Oakwood's Campus was a bridge that led to many wonderful blessings of extended joy.

Mary Lou is with longtime friends from her childhood days in Cleveland. They are standing in Blake Center, where they attended a banquet on Oakwood's University Campus. From left to right, Mrs. Dorothy Jones and her husband Elder Frank Jones standing directly behind her. Next to them is Mae Laurence, daughter of Elder JH Laurence, who pastored Mary Lou while growing up in Cleveland. Mary Lou is on the end wearing her royal blue Oakwood colors.

Elder Laurence was also the minister who baptized Mary Lou, gave her graduation commencement speech at Oakwood and he also was the very same pastor who officiated over the wedding when Mary Lou and Hugh married in 1947. Mary Lou appreciated and respected the spiritual leadership of Elder Laurence.

All three of these lifetime friends, who are shown in the previous picture, had relocated to Huntsville after their retirement. Frank Jones and Mary Lou rode the train from Cleveland to Huntsville to attend Oakwood between 1945-1947. They experienced Jim Crow segregation laws every time their train got to Cincinnati where they had to move behind the coal cars and ride for the remainder of their trip. Mary Lou said their clothes would be filled with soot by the time they arrived at Huntsville.   See the link below for more information about Elder Frank Jones:

https://www.youtube.com/watch?v=hzFesA0i0h8

It was a great blessing in so many ways that she could be surrounded by the youthful minds of a new generation while also enjoying the "old school" minds of her college days.

In the 20 years that Mary Lou spent in Huntsville, she was honored to share her faith, love and loyalty with others. She thoroughly enjoyed seeing her former students succeed and as they progressed after graduating from Oakwood. Frequently she was invited to many of her former students' weddings whenever they were taking place in Huntsville. Our Mother truly was a beautiful blessing to all of the believers that she so willingly served.

Birmingham Hillsview is sorry to hear of the passing of Ms. Heminghway. Compiled below are few fond memories of her...

Ms. Hemingway was friendly, kind and loved the Lord. She cared about the members of Hillsview and never forgot us. Even when I would see her at Oakwood, she always asked about those she remembered from Hillsview. ~ Natelka Ross Parker

I remember Ms. Hemingway as having a kind voice and sweet smile. ~ Regina Godfrey

Ms. Hemingway was a faithful pastor's wife. I vividly remember her playing the piano during a meeting we held in Lolla City. She used her talents for ministry in the church, service to the Lord and as a help meet to her husband. ~ Nathan Ross, Elder

Ms. Hemingway was a down-to-earth person. ~ Valerie Henderson

When I think of Ms. Hemingway, the words kind, loving, dedicated and Christ-like come to mind. ~ Ms. Bettye Moore

She was kindhearted and loved visiting her members. ~ Juanita Jackson

We here at Hillsview pray that you will find comfort in the promise found in 1Thessalonians 4:13-18. We plan to see Sis Hemingway again.

Comments of condolences sent from The Hillsview, Birmingham, Alabama SDA Church at the time of Mary Lou's Celebration of Life Service. She had been a well respected First Lady for the South Central Conference.

King James Bible

Thou shalt rise up before the hoary head, and honour the face of the old man, and fear thy God: I am the LORD. Leviticus 19:32

I have fought a good fight, I have finished my course, I have kept the faith: henceforth there is laid up for me a crown of righteousness, which the Lord, the righteous judge, shall give me at that day: and not to me only, but unto all them also that love his appearing. 2 Timothy 4:7-8

CHAPTER 7
Blessing Beyond Boundaries

"Accepting and Sharing Peace Despite Family Death and Terminal Cancer"

In 2003, Mary Lou found out what it was like to experience the death of a child. Marla passed away from the very same disease that had taken the life of her Grandmother Iscolar Washington, Uncle John Washington and also her father Hugh. At the time of Hugh's death in December of 1974, Mary Lou only knew that her Mother-in- law had been a stroke patient. She also knew the same about her brother- in- law, Johnny and eventually Hugh. It wasn't until Marla started asking her questions about Hugh's illness that the real cause of the Washington family's illness began to unfold.

Marla was a speech therapist within the Nashville Metro School District at the time. She started to experience signs that her Doctor felt may be M.S. (Muscular Sclerosis) As Marla's memory began to decline, her Doctor ran tests and found out that she had suffered some strokes. When she went to a specialist at Vanderbuilt, then she found out that she was probably suffering from a rare hereditary blood disorder called Antiphospholipid Syndrome.

When Marla shared the information with Mary Lou, she also followed her revelation with a host of probing questions. Just as quickly as Mary Lou was taken back to the memories of not only Hugh's illness but also Iscolar's and Johnny's, she remembered the day that one of the Cleveland church ladies had visited Mary Louise to inform her about Hugh's family illnesses. That member warned Mary Louise that Mary Lou should not marry into that family because of the sickness that apparently surrounded it. Of course Mary Louise ignored the woman's advice because she felt that Hugh had been sent by God and that he would make an absolutely fine husband for Mary Lou.

Mary Lou had been a witness to three of the Washington Family Members decline and never fully knew anything about the details of their illnesses other than their stroke diagnosis. When Marla's neurologist ran tests and compared it with the hereditary stroke history from Hugh's family, then he strongly suggested that Marla had the hereditary illness as well. Marla was very angry the day that she called Mary Lou. She could not understand why she had to be the one of her Mother's children that was suffering from her Father's hereditary illness.

Once again, after almost 30 years since Hugh's death, now Mary Lou was experiencing Marla's death. Finding herself at 75 years old and within the stages of "the golden years" of her life, was an unbelievable and surreal time to accept the role of caregiver for her 45-year-old daughter. It was also like a twisted throw back in time for Mary Lou because she was once again experiencing some of the same challenges that she had experienced with Hugh's illness. With all of that being considered, Mary Lou was also dealing with Marla's emotional highs and lows that often accompanied her daughter's "mid-life" disposition and antiphospholipid symptoms.

Marla was very blessed to have been with her Mother during a time when unpredicted sickness fell upon her. Mary Lou did not have to agree to take on the responsibility of being a caregiver at her age and also within her own home. Our Mother could have easily taken the irresponsible road and placed Marla into an assisted living facility. The fact that she did not choose that road, showed that she honored and believed in the quote that she had often shared when helping Hubert, Marla and I in our adulthood years. She would often say,

"Once a Mother, always a Mother."

That quote was not just a passing line for Mary Lou because she demonstrated it in her actions toward each of her adult children. Even in our adulthood, when we needed help from our Mother, she was intentional about helping all three of us in any way that she could.

Our Mother gave us unconditional support even in those times when she could have been like some parents and said, "I told you so, you are grown now. Figure it out on your own."

This is a picture of our beloved Mother in 1996 when she and I flew out to California from Alabama to visit Hubert in San Diego. Mary Lou was a *woman of joy* who knew how to make the most out of *any* situation in life. Mother and I had a wonderful time visiting the Battles on the west coast. It was the last time we saw her older sisters Mattie and Hazel.

When the illness of Marla's life crossed Mary Lou's path, she once again rose to the challenge and followed her own mindset regardless of the issues. Mary

213

Lou did not allow ANYTHING to deter her from seeing Marla through the same debilitating illness that she had seen Hugh through. When Marla died on July 28, 2003, Mary Lou experienced what most parents who lose children to death describe as "the worst death that a person can ever know."

My Mother never shared the depths of her grief after Marla's death. The only words that she ever shared was through this single statement,

"A parent never expects to outlive their children."

For Mary Lou, the loss of a child was harder than anyone could ever begin to imagine, because Mary Lou had to experience Marla's decline and death as a result of the same disease that had taken Hugh. That experience was an extension of grief for my Mother that brought back several memories.

Even though the boundaries of illness and caregiving had returned back to Mary Lou's life through her daughter's decline, she still continued to be a blessing not only to Marla but also to the Oakwood and Huntsville communities. Once I moved to Huntsville to share with Marla's caregiving, Mary Lou still assisted the Oakwood Dormitory Dean at Wade Hall. She willingly served as a temporary weekend, relief dean whenever she could. Helping others never left Mary Lou's heart. Regardless of the status of her situation, she always found it possible to lend a helping hand.

In the summer of 2005, Mary Lou found out that she had thyroid cancer. She had gone into Huntsville Hospital to have thyroid surgery as a result of a goiter that she had lived with for decades. During her surgery, Mary Lou's surgeon discovered cancer.

He removed as much as he could but would not risk removing the small amount that was located near her voice box. When our Mother's surgeon came out to the waiting room and told Hubert and I his findings, we both froze. Yet we could not stay in a state of shock because our 80-year-old Mother was waiting in the recovery room alone and she had already received the same information from Dr. Yerabandi, her surgeon.

Hearing that shocking word, "CANCER" can be mind changing upon its initial impact when it is coming from the mouth of your loved one's doctor. Unless you have walked in that experience you really cannot understand the dimensional race that one's mind can take when given a cancer diagnosis. The fact that it had only been two years since Marla's death did not make the diagnosis any better.

To think that after everything that Mary Lou had been through, now she was facing all of the experiences that come along with being a cancer patient. The ten weeks of radiation were some of the worst weeks of my Mother's life. It was a grueling time when her Radiologist over-radiated her throat, leaving a hole within the inside of her throat area. I WAS TOTALLY LIVID. The anger of seeing my Mother in pain was beyond words. To match that pain with the absolute negligence of Mom's Radiologist, made me even angrier. I wanted to sue that Doctor but of course Mother was not in agreement. She always believed that God would take care of *anyone* who did things that were offensively wrong. Her words of wisdom were always,

"You don't do evil for evil. Two wrongs don't make a right. Let God deal with those people. Leave it with the Lord."

Whenever Mother gave me that short sermonette, I automatically knew that there was nothing left to be said about any matter. Those words were "the last words" and Mother was not going to change her mind. With all of the determination in her heart, Mary Lou was resolutely sure that God was handling anyone who had brought harm or evil her way. She never doubted the promises of **Psalm 37: 1 *(The Lord laughs at the wicked for he sees that their day is coming.)*** *Mary Lou also claimed especially,* **Romans 8:31** *which says,*

"If God be for us, who can be against us?"

How could I debate those biblical promises when I had seen them honored in Mother's life, over and over again? Without any questions, I knew that God would have the ultimate "last word" concerning any injustices within Mother's life, even those concerning any negligence pertaining to her health-care. But in between all of the doctor visits, tests and waiting for results, were more of life's challenges that came unexpectedly and with great sorrow.

The sudden death of Oakwood's Chaplain, James Humphreys, one of our dear cousins, who had died only weeks ago from a sudden heart attack before our Mother's surgery, was also a total shock during this time.

Chaplain James Edwin Humphreys is pictured above. Jimmy, (as our family always called him) was a wonderful individual who was filled with God's Love. He was more than a blessing as the 7th Oakwood University Chaplain. *His funeral was one of the largest at the Oakwood University Church in May of 2005. Jimmy's Mother, Ernestine and Mary Lou were cousins.*

http://www.missionhuntsville.org/gdp/honor.htm

https://obits.al.com/us/obituaries/huntsville/name/james-humphreys-obituary?id=14194267

JAMES HUMPHREYS OBITUARY

May 20, 1956 May 1, 2005
Elder James Edwin Humphreys, 48, of Harvest, passed away Sunday at Huntsville Hospital. Elder Humphreys was the Chaplain of Oakwood College. Survivors include wife, Renee Humphreys; sons, Austin Humphreys, Jaren Humphreys, all of Harvest; father, Virgil Humphreys Sr.; stepmother, Bernice Humphreys, all of Flint, Mich.; mother-inlaw, Vinmor Logan of Madison; sister, Elaine Norman of Nashville; brothers, Virgil Humphreys Jr. of Berea, Ohio and Attorney Michael Humphreys of Fairfax, Vir. Visitation will be 6 to 8 p.m. today at the Oakwood College Seventh-day Adventist Church. Funeral service will be 11 a.m. Thursday at the church with Elder Leeroy Coleman officiating. Interment will be in Oakwood Memorial Gardens. In lieu of flowers, please make donations to the scholarship fund for Austin and Jaren Humphreys.

*Mary Lou is standing with her Cousin Retha Weathington, directly beside her is Mary Lou's eldest sister Daisy (Battle - Bowers} Johnson, who is standing on the right end. Cousin Retha was the Grandmother of James Humphreys, Oakwood University's 7th Chaplain. Cousin Retha lived beyond 100 years old. At the time of the picture, Mary Lou was in Detroit, Michigan traveling as a Chaperone with the Oakwood University Aeolians for one of their concerts, while they were touring. As a Residence Dean, Mary Lou enjoyed being an Aeolian Chaperone while the choir was under the direction of both Dr. Ricky Little and also Dr. Lloyd Mallory. *(See page 271 in reference to Dr. Ricky Little)*

Cousin Retha, Aunt Daisy and Mary Lou enjoyed being reunited once again.

Jimmy's death was a shock to not only the Humphreys, Weathington, Battle and Logan families, but also to the Oakwood, Huntsville and Adventist communities at large. Following his Pastoral and Youth Director assignments at the Lake Region SDA Conference in Chicago, Jimmy had been appointed as the Chaplain for Oakwood University. He had been dearly loved by so many people, young and old.

When Mary Lou received the call about his death, not too long after his heart attack, she responded almost the same way that she had decades ago when her nephew, Larry had been killed. Because Marla and Jimmy had both been born in

1956, and because of the close family ties that Ernestine (Jimmy's Mother) and Mary Lou had shared, Jimmy's death was an unbelievably shocking fact for Mary Lou.

After that great shock, Hubert and I were facing the next shocking news of our Mother's cancer prognosis. What we thought was going to be a simple surgery of removing a goiter, ended up becoming the revelation of cancer.

It was not easy facing our Mother when we were allowed to enter the recovery room. Approaching her bedside was like an unreal nightmare for me. I could not believe that Mother had cancer. As Hubert and I entered the room, I could not believe the countenance upon our Mother's face. She was peacefully smiling and then she reassuringly told both of us,

"I'm going to be alright. Don't worry. I know that God is with me."

Even in the initial moments of a cancer prognosis, while laying on her back in her recovery room, soon after her surgery, Mary Lou held firm to her mindset of faith. She was not concerned even with her own emotions, as she held her head in the direction of her adult children.

Our Mother was more concerned with the feelings of her son and daughter rather than the feelings within her own heart. In that moment, as she urged me not to cry, I was reminded again of just how unselfish my Mother had always been when it came to the best interest of her children.

Hubert and I were also challenged not to doubt God's providential will for our Mother even though she was facing cancer. As Mother firmly said,

"God is with me and He will take care of me."

something within me felt a peace and reassuring trust. I had surely seen the miracles of God manifested over and over again in our Mother's life. I had also seen God guide Mother throughout our family sorrows and difficulties. Hubert and I had to believe our Mother's Mindset because she had already shown us by her own example, exactly how God honors the prayers and obedience of his faithful children.

At 80 years of age, Mary Lou was still a strong example of courage, grace and love. The beauty of her heart far surpassed any earthly standard that had ever measured the natural beauty of her life. Our Mother had been through a host of hardships that seemed like a revolving door at times. In everything, Mary Lou still held on to the promises of faith that God had manifested to her as truth. Within the 8 decades of her life she had tried God and taken Him at His Word. Throughout all of Mary Lou's hardships, God's Word had proven to be reliable as she used it as her greatest defense.

Since the time of her early childhood, Mary Lou had been a brave soul. Even after many decades, Mother could still remember, receiving a racial slap in the face from a total stranger, while her family was visiting in Mississippi.

Shortly after arriving at my home in Louisville, one evening Mother told Hubert and I about the time she was slapped very hard in her face by a white boy who asked her,

"What are you lookin' at pick-a-ninny?"

She said that she was 5 years old at the time and did not shed one tear. When I asked her what did her parents do, she said,

"There wasn't anything that blacks could do at that time. If you were black, you better not say or do anything, if you wanted to live, especially down in Mississippi. That's just the way that it was Michelle."

From that incident of racial bigotry to this timeframe of her golden senior years, Mary Lou had learned to keep on standing, regardless of life's trouble. Cancer would not be a weapon of fear to remove her courage and faith during this time of challenge. As Mary Lou had bravely stood without tears in front of the racist teen in Mississippi, she was now also standing bravely and without tears amidst the challenges of thyroid cancer.

Mary Lou is around 5 years old in this photograph. Her bold expression reveals the tough side of her personality, even at the tender age of 5 years old.

However, cancer could not be a boundary to keep Mary Lou from blessing others. As she blessed Hubert and I within the very first moments of her cancer prognosis, she continued to bless everyone who walked into her life. She never allowed race, social or economic status, age, religion, size or shape to become a boundary between the blessing that she chose to be to bless others. Even the boundaries that were set by the intentional misdeeds of those who chose to be her enemies, could not become a boundary to Mary Lou's Mindset. If Mary Lou knew there was something that God had planned for her to do, then she did it and with all of her heart.

Another foundational part about the mindset of Mary Lou was her radiating sense of joy. I can remember when she was one of the pianists for both the Adult and Children's Division of the Sabbath School at Bethel Church. After playing the piano for the grown-ups, Mary Lou transitioned downstairs to play for the children. There she was with all of her joy motivating all of us to sing heartily, out loud.

Mother was fun and funny with her naturally animated personality. She surely was like her Mother Pearl when it came to being funny and loving music. For me, Sabbath School Song Service was like an extension from the Washington Friday night family vesper to begin the Sabbath hours. Sometimes we would sing past 11 p.m. On several occasions Mother would call our Grandmother, Mary Louise and we would sing to her. *The bond between Mary Louise and Mary Lou never lost its power.* It was easy to feel the strength surrounding their consistent love and steadfast joy.

Mary Lou and Michelle at Valley Fellowship Church in Rialto, California. It was our very last Sabbath attending that church.

The Mindset of Mary Lou was a gift from God. The way she allowed God to use her especially in times of constant hardship could be considered as totally unfathomable. Unless one looks at Mary Lou's total dependence upon God and also her total obedience to God, her Mindset seems impossible. In the final analysis of Mary Lou's Mindset, two of her favorite Bible verses can truly be aligned with her life. The first one says, *What shall we then say to these things? If God be for us, who can be against us? Romans 8:28* And the second one says, "For we know that all things work together for good to them that love the Lord and are called according to His purpose." Romans 8:32

After the initial prognosis of Mary Lou's thyroid cancer, she lived 8 more years. Always having the mindset of being a blessing to others wherever she went, made her journey one of joy. **Although Mary Lou had cancer, cancer did not have her.**

She lived beyond the boundaries of her stage 4 cancer and stage 4 osteoporosis. Despite the timelines that she was given in hospice, God allowed her to live 17 months as a hospice patient and miraculously Mary Lou surpassed each hospice timeline. Within *God's timeline*, Mary Lou fully lived each moment of every day keeping her mindset upon the promises of God's Love.

Hubert is with Mary Lou in this photo. He was visiting with her in Huntsville, Alabama. She is seen wearing her favorite rainbow colored jacket in this photo.

This picture was taken in December of 2005. Mother had been through many weeks of radiation and the Radiologist had "over radiated" her throat. You can see the darkness of her throat area around the top of her turtleneck. Regardless of her discomfort at the time, she still was filled with Christmas Joy and focused on the blessings of the season.

In the right picture, Mary Lou is pictured with her grand children, Jonathan and Danielle, Hubert's adult children. Jonathan was home from The Marines for Christmas. He treated his Nana and all of us to an Olive Garden Dinner.

This picture was taken in Redlands, California. It was in the Spring of 2009. Photography Credit: Olan Mills

Coy and Mary Lou at Emeritus Assisted Living in Loma Linda, California. Coy was also a resident at Emeritus. He was very fond of Mary Lou. They enjoyed many moments and shared many meals together, for which Coy was happy to pay for, no matter what the cost. Coy was truly a blessing and wonderful friend to Mother. He called her "Lou Lou".

Ironically enough, there was one white, apparently racist employee who was not pleased about Coy paying for Mary Lou's dinners. She even told Mary Lou this,

"Maybe Coy doesn't have the money to pay for your dinners every Friday, Mary Lou."

But after Mother told me about that remark, I wrote the Director a letter. Within the letter I asked if it was a part of that worker's job description to question my Mother like that. I can assure you that it never happened again.

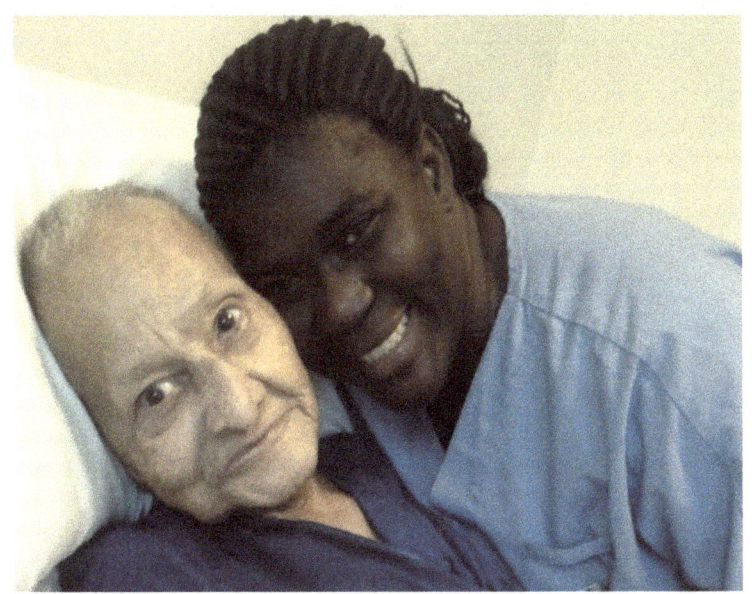

Sandra St. Gerard was Mary Lou's hospice CNA during the last months of Mother's life. She loved Mother dearly and daily called Mary Lou, "Mama". Sandra gave Mary Lou the highest service every single day. Above everything, Sandra did it with love and a smile.

Coincidentally, Sandra was also a Seventh-day Adventist just like Mary Lou.

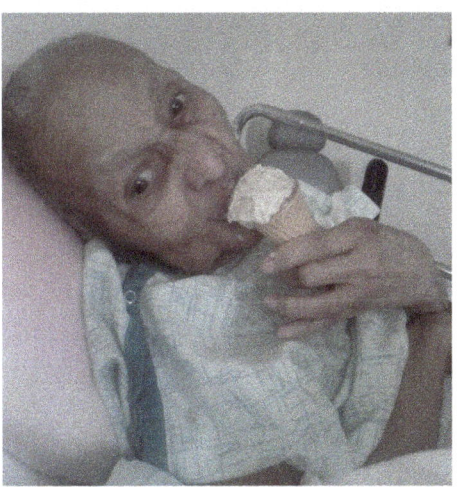

NOTHING STOPPED MARY LOU FROM ENJOYING GOOD FOOD. "SHE LOVED SOME BUTTER PECAN ICE CREAM." This picture was taken during the last few weeks of Mother's life. She ate well even up to the last night before her passing.

On August 20, 2013, Mary Lou looked at Hubert and smiled. Next, she looked at Melanie, her registered nurse from hospice and smiled. Lastly, she turned her eyes and looked at me with one of the brightest smiles that she had ever shared during her illness. Then she closed her eyes for the very last time as she took her last breath of life.

As deeply as my heart was broken, within that very same moment, I could not feel immediate sorrow. My Mother had died with the most vibrant smile upon her face and right before my presence. She had left me with a legacy of joy that transcended the worst of times. The beauty of her spirit had taught me what being "A Woman of God" was truly all about. The consistency of her prayer life had represented what a real relationship with God means. Her eager ways to share love and give to others had left me with a challenge for my own life. Whatever I had witnessed from Mother's life was filled with transparent virtues of God's Love.

How could I feel empty in any way when the Mother of my 53 years had filled my life with goodness from the depths of her own soul?

Throughout so many years she had given to everyone that she knew and even strangers that she had briefly met, the blessing of sharing her Mindset of Faith. By her very own personal example, Mother had taught Hubert, Marla and I how to face life's hardships by *leaning* upon the promises of God. **To me, that was the greatest gift and legacy of love that any parent could share with their children.** Although I wished that she could still share her grace, love and joyous faith, with the presence of her life, I knew that it was **"God's Time"** for "**Mary Lou's Mindset"** to rest.

Mary Lou and Michelle dressed alike on Mary Lou's 88th. Birthday, July 2, 2013 This was in Mary Lou's room, at Michelle's home in Louisville. The day was totally beautiful and fully blessed. It was Mary Lou's very last birthday and she enjoyed every single minute.

Within the very next month, Mary Lou passed away on August 20, 2013, exactly 4 days after Michelle's 53rd birthday.

This is a picture of the "Caramel Birthday Cake" for Mary Lou's 88th. Birthday. Caramel Cake was Mary Lou's favorite cake. Of course there was also plenty of her favorite ice cream, butter pecan. The cake was created by Kroger's Bakery.

Memories of Mary Lou

Our Mother came to Oakwood some sixty years ago.
To get her education, she left the great state of Ohio.
The trains of segregation awaited in the South.
Toward bitter lips of Jim Crow Mom had to close her mouth.
The city life of Cleveland was very far away.
Because God had a purpose, Mom had to watch and pray.
No one can quite imagine the love our Mother had.
Her loyalty to Oakwood has made her heart feel glad.
The bonds of faithful friends she made at dear O.C.,
Have lasted through her lifetime.
They've sparked her life's journey.
Mom's service at Alumni was like the morning sun,
She rose to the occasion until the job was done.
From Mr. Galley's student to a real loving Dean,
Mom loved her alma mater with service ever keen.
Mom's memories of Oakwood were memories yet unmeasured.
President Peterson and Mother Cunningham
were mentors Mother treasured.
When Mary Lou came to Oakwood her life never was the same.
Oakwood was Mother's fortune and always Mother's fame.
When the days on this earth have ended
and life here shall be no more,
Our Dear Mother will be singing
"Precious Memories" on Heaven's Shore.
Written by: Michelle L. Washington
April 20, 2004

CONCLUSION

In the *88 years* of my Mother's life I had witnessed *over half* of her joys and sorrows. During the *53 years* that I had been observing my Mother's life, I had been a witness when Mary Lou walked through the 11 years of Hugh's stroke, rehabilitation and death. Then I watched her survive the brief period of being a single woman, as a widow with two impressionable and developing daughters.

The period of witnessing Mary Lou being wooed and then married to Leroy Hemingway had to be one of the deepest and darkest valleys that I saw my Mother survive. On the other side of that was seeing Mary Lou's release, recovery and restoration after her divorce from Leroy.

It was one of the most remarkably resonant periods of her journey that I had seen in her life since my birth. Like a butterfly that transforms from the enclosure of a cocoon, I experienced the beauty of seeing my Mother transform from the dormancy of her marital separation and divorce. The miraculous vibrancy of her transformation status after divorce was truly a testimony of God's restoration power!

I had witnessed her joyous return to her beloved, Oakwood College and watched her reputation rebound beyond the rebuke that it had taken from being married to Leroy. For every defeat that Mary Lou had suffered, vibrant victories had surely followed her suffering by the amazing grace of the God that she had always trusted and honored. That in itself was the "stamp of security" which brought affirmation to Mary Lou's lifetime story.

In the darkest of days, the cruelest rejection, and even amidst the sting of intentional shunning and gossip from "*some*" of those who called themselves family and friends, I watched Mary Lou set her mind "as a flint" (stone) choosing to cling to God's promises of faithfulness. As she exercised her deepest trust in God, she mentored the example of just how much her mindset of faith mattered within her own personal journey.

What I had learned from my mother could not be purchased from any store or daily found from any other individual on the earth. Mary Lou had given me the blessing of seeing *first-hand* what it meant to have *a real Christian Mother* who *daily walked* in communion with the Lord. That was the greatest gift that she had given not only to me but also to my siblings and any other individuals whom she had shared her love for God with. No outward beauty or materialistic standards could ever equal the height of the mindset that Mary Lou had held. *She had chosen to be the woman that God had chosen for her to be and that was the defining essence of all that she desired to experience throughout her entire lifetime.*

Hubert, Marla and I were blessed to have a Mother who: shared her love for God with us, sacrificed so much for us, believed in us, individually accepted us, valued us, disciplined us, played the piano for us and sang with us, educated us, encouraged us, cooked homemade meals for us, prayed with and for us, laughed with us, shared her love for fashion and thrift stores with us, nurtured us, shared family and lifetime Oakwood friends with us, celebrated our victories with us, motivated and mentored us, traveled with us and to see us in our schools and adult homes, persevered with us and most of all unconditionally loved us even up until her very last breath.

We could not have picked out a better Mother than God gave us. Hubert and I, along with the thought of Marla's Memory, give thanks and glory to God for all the wonderful things He did through the life of our Mother, Mary Louise Battle. She was truly a woman after God's own heart who did her ultimate best to fulfill God's Will. Proverbs 31 asks,

"Who can find a virtuous woman?"

Hubert, Marla and I were able to find a virtuous one in our Mother. To God be the Glory.

This photo shows Mary Lou standing on the right of Pastor and Mrs. William DeShay in Toledo, Ohio. The rest of the Bethel S.D.A. Members in the photo are Mrs. Corrine DeShay, Mr. & Mrs. Louis Copeland. To the right of Mary Lou are Mr. & Mrs. Eddie Barnes. Seated in the front is First Elder & Mrs. Charles Wilson. The DeShays were one of the finest Pastoral couples that ever graced our Bethel Church in Toledo.

Elder William DeShay was the officiating minister for Hubert's first marriage to the former Evelyn Greenwade. What a kind and compassionate leader he was at all times.

Elder DeShay had not only been Hubert's pastor in Toledo, but also he later became Hubert's Pastor once again at Oakwood College. That was when Oakwood Church services were being held at Ashby Auditorium. Elder Deshay also drove Hubert to Pine Forge Academy when he entered there as a student in the Fall of 1963. Pastor Deshay was also the one who reassured my parents when he picked up Hubert to enroll him as a Sophomore at Pine Forge. As our pastor watched Hugh comforting Mary Lou as she was heavily crying, he empathetically said, "Don't worry Mary Lou, Corrine and I will look out for Hubert while we are in Philadelphia." The Deshays were being transferred to North Philadelphia from Toledo to Pastor their new membership. He kept his word to Mary Lou during his Ministry in Philly.

Regardless of the location, from Toledo to California, Mary Lou held close to her friends and family throughout her lifetime. In the fifth picture from left to right, Mary Lou is seen cheek to cheek with her Great Niece, Anissa Speigner who is also the Granddaughter of Mary Lou's older sister, Hazel. Anissa ("Nissa") is presently one of the greatest cooks in the Battle Family. Her Grandmother Hazel passed down a tremendous legacy of Battle Family Recipes to Nissa. In this picture, Nissa prepared some of Mary Lou's favorite dishes for her 86th birthday that was celebrated in Loma Linda, California.

Eddie and Bernice Barnes were some of the most genuine members at the Bethel SDA Church. They shared many wonderful times with Mary Lou and Hugh in Toledo.

The Barnes family kept their friendship with Mary Lou even after they moved to Springfield, Ohio and Hattiesburg, Mississippi. They made sure that they contacted and saw Mary Lou every year at South Central Conference Camp Meeting. My Mother and I had a wonderful reunion with them one summer when we went out to eat at Country Buffet in Huntsville, Alabama.

MAY · 66

Toledo SDA Faithful Church Members:
Left to right: Leona Meredith, James Hill
Virgina Pearce,(church treasurer) back
row: Mrs. Katherine Williams,
Bernice Barnes,Thelma (Williams) Atkins
Photo Credit: Marian Pearce

First Elder & Mrs. Charles Wilson
Elder Wilson was from Alabama and
he was friends with Elder Calvin Moseley
and Dr. Otis B. Edwards. (Oakwood Leaders)
Elder Wilson was a kind man who prayed
with great faith and earnest expectancy.

**The Young Adult Chorale at Parkwood (formerly Bethel)SDA Church
Left to right: Harding Owens, Hubert Washington, Evelyn Washington,
Marsha Tyson, Shyriell Owens, Mary Banks and Jim Banks. Photo credit: Dr.
Jacob Justiss**

A few Ladies of Parkwood Church: Left to right: Evelyn Washington, Essie Darnell, Shyriell Owens, Bernice Martin, Edise Scott, and sisters, Marsha (Williams)Tyson with Floella (Williams) Hyman. Photo Source: Hubert Washington

Mrs. Leona Meredith (who Hubert, Marla and I called "Grandma M."), was one of the Head Cooks at The Stranahan Mansion located on West Central Avenue in Toledo. See link for more info.:

https://metroparkstoledo.com/features-and-rentals/the-manor-house/

She was highly respected, trusted and favored by The Robert A. Stranahan Family. Robert Stranahan was the co-founder of "The Champion Spark Plug Company". Her impeccable standards of cleanliness, organization, culinary perfection and ethical service are beyond full description. In terms of her expertise, Leona Meredith could be considered to Toledo as what renown, Beverly Smith was to Washington D.C. She was a no nonsense, class act with pristine objectives. Leona Meredith was a faithful and integral part of the Bethel and Parkwood SDA Church Memberships. Her loyal friendship to Mary Lou and Hugh was forever faithful. She often sang soprano at The Allegheny Campmeeting with recording artist, Elder Charles L. Brooks. Their signature duet was, "I've Just Come From the Fountain." Listen to the link to hear performance by Kathleen Battle of the song :

https://youtu.be/Mtd6suDzjAU?si=4se8vHCj2Eocc5B

The first photo shows Mary Lou with Mrs. Dorothy Crowe and her husband, Elder Fred Crowe. Elder Crowe and Mary Lou were receiving honorary doctoral degrees in Birmingham, Alabama. Elder Crowe was the very first treasurer to serve within the SDA Regional Conferences. He was known for his standards of financial management. The second picture was taken at the Crowes Home in Hendersonville, Tennessee. Right to left is: Etta Dudley, Dorothy Crowe and Mary Lou. Mary Lou spent many happy days visiting the Crowes at their home. They treated Mary Lou just like a sister and included her adult children like family as well. It was Aunt Dorothy who *"insisted" that Uncle Fred stop in Cookeville "to check on Mary Lou" during a trip going back to Nashville with Elder and Mrs. Dudley. It was at the time that Mary Lou was awaiting her divorce from Leroy Hemingway and she was living with me during my Graduate School studies in Cookeville, Tennessee. We had a nice time with the Crowes and the Dudleys during that "check up visit". There were "some" Oakwood Faculty who felt that those who had been given honorary degrees should not have the privilege to march during the Oakwood University Commencement Weekend. Mary Lou "was not offended" by their indifference.*

Dr. Norman Miles (pictured in the first photo) grew up in Toledo and was like another son to Mary Lou and Hugh. No matter how high his attainments have been, Norman has never forgotten his humble roots in Toledo. He was always happy to see Mary Lou at camp meetings and Oakwood events. Mary Lou worked for a while at Mercy Hospital with Norman's mother. Mary Lou highly respected the legacy that "Mama Miles" built at Mercy Hospital because she had a great reputation of loving care for all the babies that were under her supervision. According to Mary Lou, "Mama Miles" could get any baby to fall asleep once they were cradled within her arms. The second picture is of Dr. Miles and his devoted and loving wife Doris (Goree) Miles. Doris has faithfully and happily been married to Norman for over 50 years. She has maintained her joy of standing by her husband since the 1960's

when Norman first brought her home to Bethel SDA Church. Dr. Norman Miles has shared his talent, skills and brilliance in many capacities within his many decades of service. He has taught as a professor at the University of Michigan and Andrews University Seminary. Dr. Miles also was one of the Lake Region Conference Presidents. His pastoral career started in Mississippi for the South Central Conference and ended when he retired in New Jersey for the Allegheny East Conference. See farewell sermon:

https://www.youtube.com/live/p1ZlgZ80V28?si=KgvToE754qVBwXPX

His awesome contributions to the development of the SDA Regional Conference Retirement Plan were stellar. Mary Lou was always proud of Norman's accomplishments and willingness to utilize and share his gifts and talents.

Elder T. Marshall and Mrs. Jean Kelly were two of Mary Lou's dearest friends whose friendships spanned all the way back to her childhood days in Cleveland. In the last photo, Mrs. Marcelle (Martin) Edmond also shared an amazing and faithful lifetime friendship with our Mother. These" forever friends" were loyal and true. Listen to the Kelly's Duet in the link.

https://youtu.be/RBNSNAeg1IM?si=g8XcMWBmlxmOEgfe

The photo above to the left is of Elder T. Marshall & Mrs. (Garland) Jean Kelly on their wedding day. See the links for more information about Elder T. Marshall Kelly.

https://youtu.be/3lEDKdNq7Lc?si=vHt5m8lvhOTXfp-v

https://youtu.be/mzRQrfZlju4?si=S2Pvbn1q6ivTIHuE

On the right is Mr. James and Mrs. Marcelle Edmond. They also were faithful friends of Mary Lou throughout her early years until their deaths.

Elder Kelly asked me to send him a letter about my Mother before her memorial service because he was doing the eulogy. I sent Elder Kelly the letter 5 days after my Mother had passed away.

At the time I was not aware of any plans to write her life story in the near future. When I recently found this letter in my old emails, a few days before sending this edit to the publisher, I realized that the letter was a preview of what this book would reveal.

See the August 25, 2013 letter below that was emailed to Elder Kelly:

me

To

tmarshallkelly@yahoo.com

Aug 25, 2013 at 10:37 PM

Good Evening Uncle Marshall,

There are so many things that I could share or say about my Mother. Her life was one filled with true faith.

Regardless of how hard or trying her tests in life were, she always found comfort in her faith that was anchored in the Lord.

I clearly remember her saying that the reason she gave her 3 children a Christian Education was because she wanted something better for them. Having attended 8 different public schools from Grades 1 through Grades 12, Mother was insistent that her children would have the blessing of educational stability and Adventist values throughout their academic experiences. She attended church school in Cleveland while in the fourth grade. It was such an enjoyable experience that she hated to have to return to public school.

Sister Frances Blake was her fourth grade teacher. Mother's memories of her one year in church school were unforgettable. Because of that one year she committed herself as a Mother to make sure that her children would have those Godly influences in school. This commitment to our development kept Mother's hands to the plow. Having a disabled husband and 3 dependent children never stopped Mother from accomplishing her goals. Through daily trusting in the Lord, she daily persevered regardless of the roughness of her journey.

She spent 12 years working for the Toledo Metropolitan Housing Authority as a bookkeeper. Her steadfastness to duty kept her faithful to her tasks. She was faithful to her professional duties, never careless, slothful or indifferent to what God placed within her hands. Her love for people and respect for their well being kept her daily attentive to the residents which dwelt within the 265 units of that public housing complex. People loved Mother because she genuinely loved them. I do not remember Mom ever being pretentious or rude. It was her customary practice to share kindness and empathy wherever she went. Her daily prayer was, "Make me a blessing to someone today." Being her caregiver for the past 18 months has been my privilege. My Mother was more than my parent, she was my friend. After having given the best of her service to her Lord, her family, her friends and church, it is only fitting that she now has time to rest from all of earth's trials and cares. My Mother was truly a woman of faith who loved God without reservation. As she walked with the Lord during 8 decades, she found a comfort in knowing that her faith was safely in God's Hands.

In closing, I echo the words of the opera singer and Oakwood Alumna, Angela Brown, "Dean Hemingway was greatly loved and will be greatly missed." Yes, I too, will miss my Mother very much but I long for that soon coming day when Jesus will come for those who are ready.

Thank you for being a faithful Christian brother and friend to our Mother. She loved you, Aunt Jean, Eric and Nadine unconditionally. I appreciate all that you have done and are doing at this time to show your concern. Continue to keep us in your daily prayers.

Love,

Michelle

(See the links to learn more about Angela Brown.) While a student at Oakwood, she resided in Carter Hall during the time Mary Lou was the Residence Dean for Carter Hall. Angela and I had a nice phone conversation after my Mother's passing. She would have loved to be a part of Mother's Memorial Service however she was out of the country at the time.

https://youtu.be/mWx_1UP0iNo?si=9JstA0mhEL3tR24V

https://youtu.be/pDZVZhlYZfA?si=lnXYVqh5gkYcE-E_

Of all of the Cleveland Friends that surrounded Mary Lou's life, Esther (Stokes) Willis was always the one that was referred to as holding the highest years of friendship. Mary Lou and Esther shared childhood memories of Mary Louise and Esther's Mother, "Sister Stokes", working closely together on many church activities. They also never forgot the childhood club that they had formed for only themselves which consisted of Esther being the President one year and Mary Lou would be the President the next year. Mary Lou and Esther also shared a lot of laughter about how Mary Lou was persistent about encouraging Esther to give Ulysess Willis "a chance" when he showed his interest to date Esther. Listening to Mary Lou paid off for Esther. She and Ulysses ended up marrying and spent a lifelong marriage of dedication, happiness and loyal unity together. They were a powerful team that mentored the highest levels of marital standards throughout their blessed union. Uncle Ullyess built a beautiful home for Aunt Esther and their 3 children, (Rosalyn, Roy and Olivia) right down the street from Pine Forge Academy. Elder Ullyess Willis faithfully served within the Allegheny East Conference Administration for many years. He was totally honest, dependable and truly wise. The next picture is of Mary Lou with Dr. Roy Willis at the Oakwood Graduation of one of Roy's sons. She was as happy as she could be.

These collages represent just a small reflection of the wonderful friends and adopted family members that surrounded Mary Lou throughout her many years of church service in Toledo, at South Central Conference and also at Oakwood University. Thanks to everyone whether you are represented in these collages or not. Your lovingkindness and loyalty to our Mother was beyond any words that can be penned. I want to especially note my deepest gratitude also to the memory of Mrs. Lorraine Miles and also to one of the current Oakwood Church Organists, Dr. Eurydice Osterman, for their wonderful leadership of the Oakwood University Church Chorale. Dr. Osterman was also my Oakwood College Choir Director. She is one of the finest musicians and directors in Oakwood's history. Our Mother thoroughly enjoyed being a member of that choir. https://youtu.be/bsK1speHeQU?si=sxiDuB-tAgt9UsKI

Pictured above in the 9th photo is Elder and Mrs. George Earle. Elder Earle (former Oakwood classmate of Mary Lou) and his wife, Vernelle were also very dear friends of Mary Lou. See the link for more info about Elder Earle. https://youtu.be/OgfbHV13n74?si=ytm3JNJ1FnWsLD8R

The Earles enjoyed many, many conversations of reminiscing and laughter on the phone throughout the 20 years that Mary Lou was a Residence Dean at Oakwood. Mrs. Vernell Earle was one of the few individuals who came to visit Mary Lou at her home during Mary Lou's 10 weeks of radiation treatments.

Whenever Mary Lou used her personal testimony of praise, by bringing her "trials to triumphs story" to the remembrance of others, she quickly reminded them of the special motto which she claimed as her sacred birthright, when she said,

"I am the 7th child, born in the seventh month."

As intentionally as it had been ordained by God that *Mary Lou had been* **born as the "7th. child",** *out of 9 Battle Children*, it was as equally and intentionally "God ordained", that when she died, she was also surrounded with seven, by the ironic fact that *Mary Lou was* **"the 7th." to die** *out of the 9 children born to Pearl and Joel Battle.* Her brothers, Henry and then Felix were the last two of her siblings to die after her death.

The third picture, (right to left) in birth order (out of nine) are Felix, Mary Lou and Henry.

Mary Lou had always believed that having God's special number upon her birth was the significantly sacred seal that had surrounded her entire life and that had also sealed her as a survivor to her every success.

As Mary Lou kept her personal story about how God's special number, "7" had held influential significance upon her entire life, she was even more amazed by how brilliantly blessed she had always been.

Mrs. Lucille Hill, one of her very best friends from college days until her death, frequently shared this statement with Mary Lou whenever they reminisced about Mary Lou's life as a survivalist, *"They cut off your feet and you kept right on walking."*

This lovely photo is of Mrs. Lucille (Elmond Jackson) Hill. Mrs. Hill was the wife of Elder Franklin Hill, Sr. Together they served all over the United States as a faithful Pastor and Teacher Team for the SDA Church. They were both graduates of Oakwood and classmates of Mary Lou. Mrs. Hill was one of Mary Lou's dearest friends. Photo credit: Sherry Salla (2011 Find a Grave)

As they enjoyed the laughter about that statement, they both knew that God had truly kept my Mother walking. Though they shared a lot of laughter about this, they were grateful for the reality of God's Goodness toward Mary Lou.

Dr. Michael and Terry Harris were loyal friends to Mary Lou while she was experiencing the beginning of Leroy Hemingway's affair in Knoxville. Terry is the daughter of Elder Franklin Hill, Sr. and Mrs. Lucille Hill. Terry and Mike drove from Indiana and spent an entire weekend with my Mother and I, in Louisville. Their devotion to my Mother was truly faithful and unforgettable.

I cannot ever fully thank all of those known and unknown individuals who stood by my Mother in her times of difficulty throughout the 88 years of her life. To name some, would be a rebuke and an offensive oversight to those left unnamed. So, to all of you who were warriors on behalf of Mary Lou Battle (Washington) Hemingway, during the dark days of her deepest difficulties, I say a huge THANK YOU! Were it not for the fact that you allowed God to use you in "a time of trouble" for our Mother's best interest, she may not have been able to be the survivor that she was. You all were like the text in the Bible which refers to "a friend that sticks closer than any brother."

To Al and Carolyn Fairley of Perris, California,

I must release this statement before I close the pages of this book.

Carolyn and Albert Fairley are pictured standing behind Mary Lou at Emeritus Assisted Living in Loma Linda California. They were her exceptionally adopted California Children and "Angels" in my absence.

You both were the children that my Mother did not birth, but that she surely accepted, trusted and cherished. When Mother's cancer returned for the second time and when she knew that she was approaching what soon would be her last and final years, you both stepped up and stood by her side while I was trying to secure employment and a home to bring her to on the East Coast. When the devilish lies, schemes and attacks of those who were being used to bring discord occurred, I tremendously thank Carolyn for being the one who immediately informed me of the urgency to move my Mother from California as soon as possible. Carolyn, you were the main individual that God used to give Mary Lou Hemingway hope so that she could have the opportunity of living once again with me, her daughter.

With that bold decision of standing as a warrior in her defense, you allowed her the privilege of not only living with the sense of security of being around her own children, but also, you provided her with the opportunity of dying in peace while also in the presence of her children.

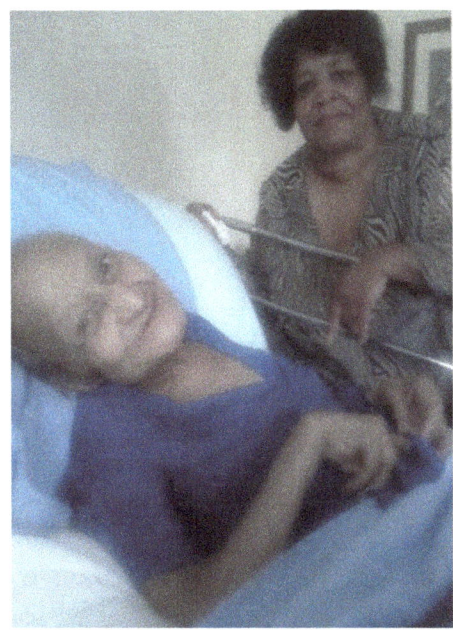

Ella Minor was the Louisville Angel that unashamedly petitioned Pastor Kennedy Luckett for funds from the church to cover the airline flights to bring my Mother to Louisville from Loma Linda.

To the memory of Ms. Ella Minor, (now deceased), I will always be grateful for her boldness in being the Louisville warrior that approached Pastor Kennedy Luckett about transporting my Mother, by plane, from California to Louisville. Miss Ella knew that I would not have ever chosen to take that path. That's why she made it for me without initially informing me of her intentional course of action. She also invited her sister, Mary Minor to be the driver to take me to the airport. I'm thankful to Mary for so willingly consenting. In addition, Pastor Luckett's consent to allow the church to financially assist in that emergency endeavor was critical toward making this final transition for Mary Lou's life. *His choice to request for that consent will always be appreciated and remembered with great gratitude by Hubert and I.*

This is a picture of Mary Lou with Pastor Kennedy Luckett and his wife, First Lady Veronica Luckett. This was one of the times when Pastor and Mrs. Luckett stopped by our home to see Mom on Sabbath, after Church. Mother truly respected the faithfulness that Pastor Luckett shared with her in this season of her final cancer stage.

This photo was taken September 11,2001 (9-11). Mary Lou is standing next to Edward (Eddie) Green. He was in Huntsville for his Uncle Willie Tramel's Funeral.

Eddie was the one who fed Mother her very last dinner on August 19, 2013. Eddie was also the one who had told her not to leave Rochester, New York before she went back with Leroy Hemingway and moved to Pensacola, Florida in 1986.

In 1987, it was Eddie who drove Mother and I to Nashville, Tennessee where she met with the Conference Committee, by "their invitation". There she was asked to share her story.

Again, in the Spring of 2007, Eddie Green was the one who flew into Huntsville and escorted my Mother and I to "her" 60th College Reunion and "my" 25th College Reunion at Oakwood University.

It was Eddie who accompanied Mother "everywhere" she desired to go while in her transport chair. She enjoyed seeing all of her friends and family members that Easter Weekend. What a wonderful time we had. We had a "double celebration" during that Alumni Weekend because Mary Lou was a graduate of the "Class of 1947" and I was a graduate of the "Class of 1982." It was the "very last" Alumni Weekend that my Mother and I attended.

Like another son, Eddie called Mary Lou, "Mom". He defended her many times when she and I were having our Mother-Daughter issues. At times he was quick to tell me, "Michelle, Mom is right."

Eddie was one of very few people who could hold opposing conversations, which were at times, not in agreement with Mary Lou's Mindset and strong opinions. Eddie was able to fully keep Mother's attention and make his point because she often respected Eddie's viewpoints.

The involvement of all of these people proved to be providential for so many reasons because Mary Lou died in Kentucky, the very same state where she had been born in 1925. She had returned to her place of origin to close the final stages within the last 1 year and 7 months of her life.

This story about my Mother's Mindset only touches the surface of her story. If I had fully recorded all of the experiences that she had shared with me as well as all of the ones that I had witnessed, her story would have never been finished. In the final analysis, it was of most importance to share inspirational glimpses of Mary Lou's Mindset that propelled her past frustration, fatigue and failure to faith.

It is my prayer that the readers of this story have been influenced in a way that has led them even closer to the God of Heaven who watches over all of us every single day.

May we all be a part of those who hear the words of Jesus, found in Matthew 25:21, when our Lord and Savior returns for his redeemed.

"His lord said unto him, well done, thou good and faithful servant: thou hast been faithful over a few things, I will make thee ruler over many things: enter thou into the joy of thy lord."

This is a picture of Mother's Gravesite which is located at Oakwood University Memorial Gardens Cemetery in Huntsville, Alabama.

The photo below is located on the very last page of the 1946 Oakwood Yearbook. Mary Lou is seen leaning on the pillar with her classmates. Her love for her Alma Mater never wavered or grew cold throughout the decades.

How appropriate that she is buried on the very grounds (Oakwood Memorial Cemetery Gardens) where she spent some of her happiest days. As a student, dormitory residence dean, relief dean, volunteer receptionist for student health services and the development office, alumni weekend registration volunteer, church chorale member, church hospitality receptionist, and church member, Mary Lou shared her love for her beloved college and church in any way that she could. We look forward to reuniting with our beautiful and beloved Mother when Jesus returns at His Second Coming. Then we will experience with her the reality of one her favorite Oakwood Songs, entitled, "A City of Light". https://youtu.be/fdTsk2ncitk

From her 1947 Oakwood Graduation on to her service as an Oakwood Residence and Relief Dean and also the conferring of her Honorary Doctoral Degree, Mary Lou had gone full circle with the blessings of God's special number "7" upon her life. She experienced God's Goodness continuously as a woman who had chosen a Godly Mindset and Lifestyle. Mary Lou left her legacy of leadership, loyalty and love for the next generations.

OAKWOOD UNIVERSITY HISTORICAL AND
BACKGROUND INFORMATION

(Also Special Credits)

YOUTUBE VIDEO Credits

Black SDA History You tube Channel*

1. "A Call to Mission" A History of Oakwood University

https://youtu.be/WjDVldcVV0Q

2. Oakwood History

https://youtu.be/ZUnaLCj78vl

Special thanks to our "Cousin Turner" for Oakwood 1946 and 1947 reference information and phone interviews with him. {Dr. Turner Battle, III}

SPECIAL CREDITS LIST

I DO NOT OWN THE RIGHTS TO ANY OF THE YOU TUBE VIDEO LINKS THAT ARE POSTED THROUGHOUT *Mary Lou's Mindset.* Individual credits for each video is posted with each author's name as seen upon the videos. The videos have been shared solely to provide additional information about individuals, contributors and their relationships to Oakwood and the content of this historical life story.

I DO NOT OWN THE RIGHTS TO ANY MUSIC OR SHARED DOCUMENTATION ON YOU TUBE VIDEOS, OBITUARY PROGRAMS, NEWSPAPER OR MAGAZINE ARTICLES, BOOK EXCERPTS OR RELATED PHOTOS.

A LARGE AMOUNT OF PHOTOS CONTAINED IN *Mary Lou's Mindset* are a part of her own personal photos taken throughout various time periods and events in her life.

Mr. Lucian Dixon, (deceased) professional photographer and family friend has been credited for Hugh and Mary Lou's wedding photos, as well as other pictures that are noted throughout the book.

Special notes of reference credits: *Dr. Benjamin Baker, You tube, *Black SDA History Videos* (see following link about Dr. B. Baker)

https://www.youtube.com/watch?v=LqZm5H-dP8g

Also see his website, https://www.blacksdahistory.org/about

Mrs. Minneola Dixon, former Oakwood University Archivist for The Eva B. Dykes Library, Loma Linda Article. *Faces of Oakwood*, You tube Links are provided solely as additional points of reference for educational purposes. (*Credits: Oakwood University's Office of Marketing & Public Relations Office.)*

Mr. Alex Hayes, Scored music for *"Only God Can".*

The credits are in alphabetical order by last names of individuals listed.

ELDER MAURICE BATTLE

*Additional information for page 59

https://youtu.be/gV11g9w7fdI

https://adventist.news/news/former-adventist-world-church-associate-secretary-dies-at-82

DR. TURNER C. BATTLE, III

*Additional information for page 59

Creator & Artist of Oakwood University Seal

August 28, 2024, 7 p.m. Phone Interview with Dr. Turner Battle, (now 98 years old), Regarding the Oakwood Seal Origin Dr. Battle's Shared Account is Documented Below :

"When I returned to Oakwood from EMC, Emmanuel Missionary College, (now Andrews University), James Dykes and I were talking and I told him that Oakwood didn't have a Yearbook. Shortly after that conversation, President Peterson called me to his office.

He told me that his daughter, Marjorie, had an EMC Yearbook that had me listed as the Art Editor. Then President Peterson asked me if I had been requested to be their Art Editor. I then explained that the EMC Students had voted for me to be their 1945 Art Editor. After the conversation, President Peterson requested for me to be the 1946 Art Editor for Oakwood's first and 50th Anniversary Yearbook. James Dykes was the Editor.

I started working on the seal. It was a difficult task. I did not finish the seal before the yearbook was printed. That's why there is an empty circle on the front cover of the yearbook where the seal was going to be placed.

When I finished the seal and showed it to President Peterson, he asked me to explain what it represented. I told him the scroll represented the Bible, the feathered pen was a symbol for Mrs. Ellen G. White's Writings and the torch represented all the generations of Oakwood Students sharing the Bible and Mrs. White's Writings with others. After I finished talking, President Peterson went to the window and thought for a few minutes. Shortly after thinking about it, he then looked at me and said, I like that. We will use this for our seal.

The seal was first published on the front cover of The 1947 Oakwood Course Catalog. I still have a copy of that catalog. I gave Oakwood the actual drafting pens and instruments that I used when I created the seal. I also gave them the story of how the seal was developed. Everything I gave regarding The Oakwood Seal should be there in the Library Archives.

James Dykes was a good writer. That is why he was selected as the Editor for the 1946 Yearbook. He and I found old slides behind the Print Shop. We salvaged them and used them to create that Anniversary Annual. Later on we met and decided upon naming the Yearbook, The Acorn. It was also decided to have a school newspaper and that it would be called, The Spreading Oak. Although James Dykes was the editor for the 1946 Oakwood Yearbook, in 1950, I was the Oakwood Yearbook Editor.

I had an early interest in drawing and art. In 1938 or 39, I was in the 9th Grade. I took a cartooning class and learned about developing cartoons. I wanted to go to The Art Institute in Chicago. My Dad wanted me to go to Oakwood. In 1938 or 39, I published my first cartoon. It was for the NAACP, CRISIS MAGAZINE. The cartoon showed a negro being squeezed in a metal vice. I won the competition and that is how the cartoon was published."

DR. EARL E. CLEVELAND

*Additional information for pages 124-126

Related links from articles

https://encyclopedia.adventist.org/article?id=CCEG

https://spectrummagazine.org/article/jared-wright/2009/09/01/evangelist-and-administrator-e-e-cleveland-dies

https://en.m.wikipedia.org/wiki/E._E._Cleveland

You tube related links

https://youtu.be/garjkD0myUk   https://youtu.be/AJObBaFxUvQ

https://youtu.be/XRG1LULczbo   https://youtu.be/cU-Q8ly23FE

Some of the books Dr. Cleveland wrote: Bradford Cleveland Brooks Institute

below:

MRS. EUGENIA CUNNINGHAM
*Additional information for page 100

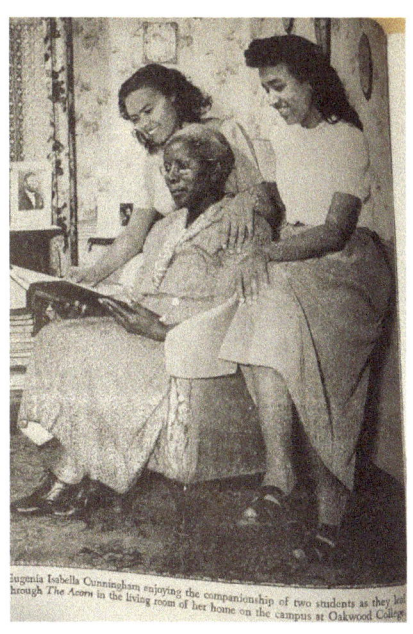

Picture from "Make Bright the Memories

Biography of Mrs. Eugenia Cunningham
https://encyclopedia.adventist.org/article?id=DHE7

Picture of Cunningham Hall

DR. CHARLES EDWARD DUDLEY
*Additional information for page 203

https://youtu.be/C01AyTvdAXY

You tube related links:

https://youtu.be/vS0cswk3ODE

Related links of articles:

https://encyclopedia.adventist.org/article?id=7CEK

Some of the books written by Dr. Charles Edward Dudley:

https://youtu.be/OSdjQEJXIBQ?si=YnZsDPYtmmX8s1Ue

DR. EVA B. DYKES

*Additional information for page 153

Related links for articles about Dr. Dykes:

https://spectrummagazine.org/news/2018/eva-beatrice-dykes-first-african-american-woman-complete-phd-requirements

https://legacyofslavery.harvard.edu/alumni/eva-beatrice-dykes

https://kentakepage.com/eva-beatrice-dykes-the-first-black-woman-to-fulfill-the-requirements-for-a-doctoral-degree/

Related You Tube Links about Dr. Dykes:

https://youtu.be/qaf5gFURq8s

https://youtu.be/6Ai-TZF3mtw   https://youtu.be/sERJGvH9njY

https://youtu.be/onzauDnPoV8 https://youtu.be/CLd8XVHbNLw

MR. ART EDGERTON

*Additional information for page 159

TRIBUTE TO ART EDGERTON

————

HON. MARCY KAPTUR

of ohio

in the house of representatives

Monday, October 23, 2000

Ms. KAPTUR. Mr. Speaker, I wish to pay tribute to an extraordinary man from my district, Mr. Art Edgerton. Art unexpectedly passed from this life on Tuesday, September 26, 2000 in his home in Perrysburg, Ohio. Art exemplified artistry, humanitarianism, and zest in every aspect of his being.

Well known to Northwest Ohioans, Art was a most talented and accomplished musician who made his mark nationwide. Though he began his professional career as a drummer at the tender age of nine, Art's piano playing was legendary and he played with various bands through the early 1950s. Even after settling in Toledo, Ohio and pursuing other employment, Art continued playing the piano, entertaining audiences in his adopted hometown.

In 1957, Art entered into a new career, that of broadcasting. Beginning as a part time disc jockey with the former WTOL radio station, he soon transitioned to a report for both radio and television covering civic affairs. Art broke into this field at a time when his race and his disability made this pursuit very difficult. Still he persevered, enduring prejudice with grace, covering the 1963 March on Washington and, blind since birth, taking notes in Braille. An early colleague best summed up Art's style: `` . . . a very accomplished reporter. He was extremely sensitive at a time when being a black reporter presented him with a lot of obstacles.'' The colleague noted how it was not easy for many people to accept Arts' use of Braille writing as he reported an event, and highlighted ``Art's ability to maintain his composure and to deal fairly with everyone he dealt with, even if they didn't deal fairly with him.'' Even as he continued in his journalism and music careers, Art took on a new challenge in the late 1960's becoming an administrative assistant in the external affairs office of the University of Toledo and later, the Assistant Director for Affirmative Action.

Active in community affairs as well, Art served as Board President of the Ecumenical Communications Commission of Northwest Ohio, Board Member of the Greater Toledo Chapter of the American Red Cross, member of the President's Committee on Employment of the Handicapped, President of the Northwest Ohio Black Media Association, and the National Association of Black Journalists. In 1995 he was inducted into that organization's Regional Hall of Fame. Among all of his awards and accolades, Art was perhaps most proud of receiving the 1967 Handicapped American of the Year Award which was presented to him personally by Vice President Hubert Humphrey. Coming from an unhappy childhood in which his parents could not accept his blindness, his wife explained why this particular award affected him so deeply, ``With his upbringing, how he had to scuffle, he just figured he would never be recognized. The fact that somebody recognized what he done gave him that much more determination to continue and do better.''

Mr. Speaker, Art Edgerton was a friend and a trusted advisor throughout the years I have served in this House. I shall miss deeply, as will our entire community. He made us better through his caring and talents spirit. He always advocated for the rights of people with disabilities. Exceedingly gracious, completely endearing, unfailingly honest, yet with a core of steel, Art Edgerton was a man among men. We offer our profoundest and heartfelt condolences to his wife of 35 years, Della, his sons Edward and Paul, his grandchildren and great-grandchildren. May their memories of this truly great man carry them forward.

HISTORIC IMAGES

1967 Press Photo VP Humphrey presents Handicapped American award to Art Edgerton

This is an original press photo. Art Edgerton, blind newsman and music director at a Toledo, Ohio television station, was honored today as "The Handicapped American for 1966." Vice-President Hubert Humphrey presented the award in Washington. Edgerton, a native of Philadelphia is an excellent pianist and organist. Photo measures 10 x 8 inches. Photo is dated 04-27-1967.

PHOTO FRONT

Photo Credits for Art Egerton's picture. (Page 160)

Watch you tube link below to see Art Edgerton honored with wife Della.

https://youtu.be/WOSJNrNZvWI

Dr. Frank Hale Jr. was president of Oakwood College from 1966 until 1971. (Courtesy of The Ohio State University)

DR. FRANK HALE

*Additional information about Dr. Hale for page 144

.Related links for articles about Dr. Hale:

https://rb.gy/1p515j

https://kb.osu.edu/handle/1811/5779

https://youtu.be/zxqm5RSkBe4

https://youtu.be/BHsRvK4JUUY

https://www.youtube.com/watch?v=h5AHi1iYOyQ

https://youtu.be/asy4uzaUGOo

Ohio State University, Columbus, Ohio

https://youtu.be/IT0RcZZNVCM

Hale Hall, location of Dr. Frank Hale, Jr. Cultural Center

DR. JACOB JUSTISS

*Additional information for page 124

https://encyclopedia.adventist.org/article?id=5CEY&highlight=Pita%7CManu

https://adventistregionalministries.org/the-long-awaited-republication-of-angels-in-ebony/

Dr. Jacob Justiss often came to Toledo to visit his sisters who were stellar teachers within the Toledo Public School System. Mrs. Juanita Hill, sister of Dr. Justiss is pictured with her son, Vincent in the second picture. Dr. Justiss was a man of brilliance, eloquence and risk taking. As an amazing trailblazer, he was completely unafraid to bring total truth to the forefront regardless of public approval. His contributions were truly cutting edge. He waa a genuine friend to Hugh and Mary Lou throughout the years.

Photo Credit: From the Personal Photos of Vincent Hill, Nephew of Dr. Jacob Justiss.

Angels in Ebony

by

Jacob Justiss

uld be told.

When E.E. Cleveland graduated from Oakwood Junior College, his throat s so bad that the Ministerial Department would not recommend him. He sisted as a janitor in Toledo, Ohio, in the home of Brother David

—110—

Washington, the local colporteur. When W.R. Robinson tried to pave his into the Ohio Conference, W.H. Robbins listened and shook his h Cleveland's faith, though shaken, held and was considerably strengthed by marriage to Celia Abney, who had rejected another very promising minist prospect. 1946 found the Cleveland's in Greensborough, North Carc blessed with 113 souls. The two associates, Eric Ward and Warren Banf left to try their wings. But Cleveland against the advice of the Conference that God wanted another effort in Greensboro. Without a conference bud he moved to the other side of town and God blessed with 114 souls.

Soon others began to ask how it was done and Cleveland mimeographe sermons - sermons which included many all-time greats proven succes through the years, but also a new type sermon - sermons with the bui psychology of soul winning — Cleveland's own vintage. Then appe "Questions and Answers" with this new "in," anticipating step by step inner needs of the seeker of truth, forming the need into a question supplying the faith - anchoring answer. This technique added to Mrs. Cl land's extra-ordinary piano playing and new departure in Bible work plus encouraging innovations of piling the baptismal garments, bundles, in the as visible evidence of decisions added greatly to the thrill of the approac "big baptism" which usually occurred.

In June 1954, Cleveland was elected to the General Conference Minist Department and at age 33 was at that time the youngest man to move that august body. Since then he has taught his methods by precept

The Aeolians of 1994, under the direction of Ricky Little.

DR. RICKY LITTLE

*Additional Information for page 218

Pictured above in the front row, far right is, Dr. Ricky Little, who appreciated Dean Hemingway accompanying the Aeolians on overnight and out of town promotional trips for Oakwood.

In the email below, Dr. Little shared his sentiments about Mary Lou's dependability. Dr. Little shared this to be read at Mary Lou's Celebration of Life Service which was held at Oakwood University Church, September 5, 2013. The You tube clip shows the Aeolians during

Dr. Little's leadership.   https://youtu.be/gKubZeHL0iM

A Tribute to Your Mom:

I only chose people I could trust, those who put Christ first, and put themselves last. Those who lived by true Christian example, exemplifying the King's standards and not their own. Those whose hearts were filled with love for His children, and knew how to present and represent Christ to those under their charge. Those through whom the light of the Holy Spirit shown, so that our students could see a brighter and better way. Those who I thought God trusted, and thus I had no fear that our students and I could also trust. Those who put self out of the picture and allowed Christ to shine in a way that no one was confused. When I needed a friend, a colleague, a trusted counselor, a beautiful spirit, a person of warmth and genuine love, a sister in Christ to help me with my responsibilities of chaperoning the Aeolians on trips and in life, I chose Dean Hemingway. And like you, it will be my great joy to see her again in the Kingdom of God. In closing, I leave you with God's commendation to His precious child:

"Behold my servant, whom I have chosen; my beloved, in whom my soul is well pleased". Matthew 12:18

With my love,

Ricky Little

271

ELDER FRANK L. PETERSON
Third President of Oakwood University
* Additional information for page 101

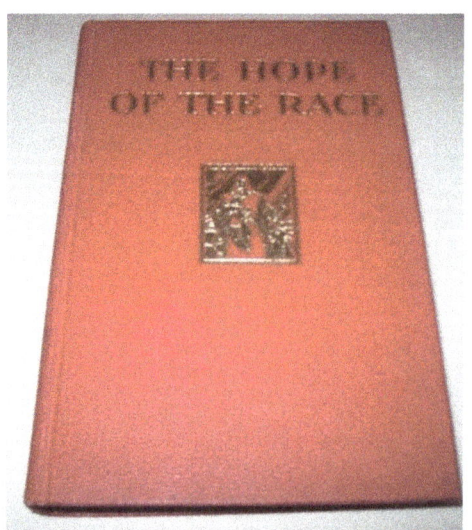

FRANK LORIS PETERSON
The Author

THE NORTH AMERICAN INFORMANT

A BIMONTHLY REPORT OF THE NORTH AMERICAN REGIONAL DEPARTMENT

VOLUME XXIV   WASHINGTON, D.C., JANUARY-FEBRUARY, 1970   NUMBER 1

Frank Loris Peterson

(1893-1969)

FRANK LORIS PETERSON was born in Pensacola, Florida, August 12, 1893, and passed to his rest on October 23, 1969, in Los Angeles, California. He was the youngest of four children born to devout Methodist parents, Frank and Elizabeth Peterson. Frank received his elementary and high school education in private Methodist schools, where at an early age he displayed an unusual aptitude and proficiency in his academic studies and in music.

At the tender age of fourteen, while in high school, he was privileged to hear the dynamic preaching of Elder J. H. Laurence. Though just a young lad, Frank Loris Peterson responded to the tender pleadings of the Holy Spirit and gave his heart to God, and in 1907 was baptized by Elder Laurence into the Seventh-day Adventist Church. Those who knew him could see in Frank the characteristics and potential for being an outstanding worker in the cause of God and encouraged him toward the ministry.

He entered Pacific Union College as a theology student and in 1916 became the first "man of color" to graduate from this Seventh-day Adventist college located on beautiful Howell Mountain in northern California. Immediately after his graduation, he was invited to assist Elder P. G. Rogers in Baltimore, Maryland, for a brief period.

That autumn he became a teacher in the church school at Louisville, Kentucky. In September of 1917 he accepted an invitation to teach at Oakwood Junior College in Huntsville, Alabama, and served there until 1926. He left Oakwood to become assistant MV, educational, and home missionary secretary for the old Southern Union of Seventh-day Adventists, with headquarters in Nashville, Tennessee, and held this position until 1929. In that year he was ordained to the ministry in Nashville, Tennessee.

Elder Peterson became pastor of the Berea church in Boston Massachusetts, in January of 1929 and continued in this capacity until July of 1930. In 1930 he was chosen as secretary of the North American Negro

Department of the General Conference of Seventh-day Adventists and he served in this position until 1941. He then accepted an appointment as pastor of the Wadsworth church of Los Angeles, California, from 1941 until 1945. In 1945 he became president of Oakwood College in Huntsville, Alabama, and served in that capacity until 1954.

In 1954 at the forty-seventh World Conference of the church Elder Peterson was nominated as an associate secretary of the General Conference of Seventh-day Adventists and secretary of the Regional Department of the General Conference. In 1962 the same body elected him a vice-president of the denomination, the first Negro to hold such a position. The world was his parish.

He married Bessie Jean Elston on May 3, 1922, at Anniston, Alabama. They became the parents of five children. They are: Frank L. Peterson, Marjorie E. Knight, Calvin E. Peterson (now deceased), Katherine E. Palmer, and Clara E. Rock.

In 1966 at the General Conference session in Detroit, Michigan, Elder Peterson retired from the active ministry but not from service for his Lord. After moving back to California, he and Sister Peterson, in spite of considerable physical suffering, continued to serve the cause of God willingly and unselfishly whenever called upon to do so. Up until the time that death came, he never ceased to show interest and concern for the young people of the church and for Christian education.

Truly a courageous soldier has fallen—a soldier who companioned with his Commanding General and followed his orders explicitly; a soldier who did not flinch in the heat of battle; a soldier who did not retreat when confronted by the enemy; a soldier who fought a good fight and finished the course; a soldier who kept the faith when it was not always easy; a soldier who now awaits the reward which the Commanding General shall give to those who endure unto the end.

Frank Loris Peterson

President Peterson was a man of distinction, integrity and honor. Mary Lou valued his stellar leadership while enrolled as a student at Oakwood.

PRINCIPAL FLUTE RICE

*Additional information for page 112

https://www.toledoblade.com/news/deaths/2006/08/14/Scott-High-s-1st-African-American-principal-took-helm-after-60s-riots/stories/200608140029

There are few who have made contributions within the educational realm of Toledo, Ohio as those of Principal Flute Rice. Administratively, Mr. Flute Rice was an educational icon in Toledo. His legacy will forever be remembered as monumental towards implementing, maintaining and balancing standards of equity and inclusion within the Toledo Public School System. His legendary influence at Scott High School was beyond stellar.

DR. ERNEST E. ROGERS

Additional information for page 145

https://www.waff.com/2021/06/18/retired-oakwood-professors-secret-105-years-life-stay-happy/?outputType=amp

https://m.facebook.com/photo.php?fbid=1733866636817144

https://obits.al.com/us/obituaries/huntsville/name/ernest-rogers-obituary?id=31543830

https://youtu.be/2hxTCIS97AM?si=LsoIbtkP_R5IYzv2

The legacy that Dr. E.E. Rogers left Oakwood has influenced many generations of pastors who took Greek under his brilliant instruction. None can truly measure the vast influence that Dr. Rogers had upon the Religion and Theology Department at Oakwood University. Dr. Rogers also taught other religion courses that were required for education majors and entering students who had not graduated from Adventist High Schools. Because he was always a man of kindness, keenness and laughter, he was a favored instructor. His classes were interesting, enlightening and enjoyable.

ELDER DAVID WASHINGTON

Additional information for page 125

One of the First Founders of Toledo Bethel SDA Church, Ohio Conference Colporteur

SEE PAGE 285 ***BELOW OF ELDER LOUIS B. REYNOLD'S BOOK, "We Have Tomorrow"

Elder Reynolds was a former editor for the Message Magazine.

Elder Washington was also instrumental in building up the membership in the SDA Beacon Light Church in Phoenix, Arizona. His final church was Juniper Avenue SDA Church in Fontana, California. David Washington was a man of fervent daily prayer.

See the link for one of Elder Washington's favorite hymns:

https://youtu.be/iXQoPTn5-PQ?si=LJLgv15-IjoOvX4L

TO THE CITIES OF THE EAST   285

In 1916 the family moved to Millington, Tennessee, a suburb of Memphis. Among others to whom Joe Hudson gave Bible studies was one David Washington. Washington joined the church in Memphis but later moved to Toledo, Ohio. Because he could find no church in Toledo, he began immediately contacting prospects and giving Bible studies. Before long several people were ready for baptism, and these formed the nucleus of the present Toledo congregation.
                                    in 1918. There R.

Elder Washington also opened his home in Toledo to Earl E. Cleveland for a year after his graduation from Oakwood, when no regional conference offered him a pastorate.

ENTERTAINER ETHEL WATERS

*Additional information for page 44

Ethel Waters Singer Actress 1st African-American Woman Nominated for Emmy Award

INFORMATION SOURCE: EBAY

Photo Reproductions

Black History

TITLE: Ethel Waters Singer Actress 1st African-American Woman Nominated for Emmy Award

Description: Ethel Waters, in a photo by William P. Gottlieb believed to have been taken in New York City, N.Y - Ethel Waters (October 31, 1896 -September 1, 1977) was an American blues, jazz and gospel singer and actress. She frequently performed jazz, big band, and pop music, on the Broadway stage and in concerts, but she began her career in the 1920s singing blues.
Her best-known recordings include "Dinah," "Stormy Weather," "Taking a Chance on Love," "Heat Wave," "Supper Time," "Am I Blue?" and "Cabin in the Sky," as well as her version of the spiritual "His Eye Is on the Sparrow." Waters was the second African American, after Hattie McDaniel, to be nominated for an Academy Award. She was also the first African-American woman to be nominated for an Emmy Award, in 1962.

**ARTICLE ABOUT ETHEL WATERS AND BILLY GRAHAM CRUSADES

https://billygrahamlibrary.org/exhibit-to-honor-legendary-performer-ethel-waters/

LETTER OF AUTHENTICITY

This photograph which has been autographed by Ethel Waters came from the Estate of Clark Gesner, the composer and lyricist whose defining success was the 1967 smash You're a Good Man, Charlie Brown. Mr. Gesner (1938-2002) began collecting in 1956 when he obtained the autograph of Clark Gable. From there, he built a collection of more than 10,000 autographs. He obtained the autographs in person, from autograph dealers, or by mail. Mr. Gesner was a well-known collector and shared his collection with Brooklyn Heights area churches, schools, senior citizen groups and other organizations.

First and foremost I evaluate the flow of the signature. I also look for the speed of the signature and then I'll start looking for the formation of the letters. I will ascertain pen pressure, hesitations, stops, skips,patches, line quality, connecting strokes, 'i' dots, "t" bars, and baseline writing. If I'm looking at line quality, I'm looking for tremor in the line quality. Has the ink permeated the paper or does it sit on top of the fibers just recently applied? Does the ink used for the signature match the time period. Modern pencil drawings have graphite shine until they oxidize. Modern paper deteriorates and becomes more brittle. Brown mildew spots appear called foxing. Microscopic analysis can tell if the signature was applied recently on old paper on top of the old foxing.

The autograph was also evaluated using standard nondestructive techniques of forensic document examination which include a macroscopic evaluation (with the naked eye) with calipers, protractors, photocopies and their enlargements,along with computer enhancements and computer enlargements. I do side-lighting to check for indented writing to see if there was pressure on the instrument. The signature is consistent with other exemplars that I have examined.

Memorabilia Autographs

This is verification of Ethel Waters signature authenticity on photo located on page 40.

YOU TUBE VIDEOS OF ETHEL WATERS

https://youtu.be/X4UbSngOA_A

https://youtu.be/Df3P4cO4Co0

https://youtu.be/3y4iYLc6xkY

**OAKWOOD FOUNDERS
1896**

The founders of Oakwood–O. A. Olsen, president of the General Conference of Seventh-day Adventists; G. A. Irwin, superintendent of the Southern Region; and Harman Lindsay, former treasurer of the General Conference–stood near the gateway to the old Beasley Estate as they surveyed the property that was to become the Oakwood Industrial School. With the support of Ellen G. White, was purchased from the owner, Michael O'Shaughnessey.

Oakwood Historical Site

ELLEN GOULD WHITE

Author, Prophetess, Oakwood Founder

Leader of SDA Church

*Additional information from pages 22 & 94

Related Links

https://m.egwwritings.org/en/about

https://m.egwwritings.org/en/book/435.62

https://spectrummagazine.org/article/benjamin-baker/2011/02/08/how-oakwood-became-mecca-black-adventism

You tube links

https://youtu.be/k_oA849HMLE

https://youtu.be/uoyJQU0IoNs

https://youtu.be/_2Iik6b7IDY

https://youtu.be/bOnZgmlSvBM?si=nEhD_-u92FFedtiE

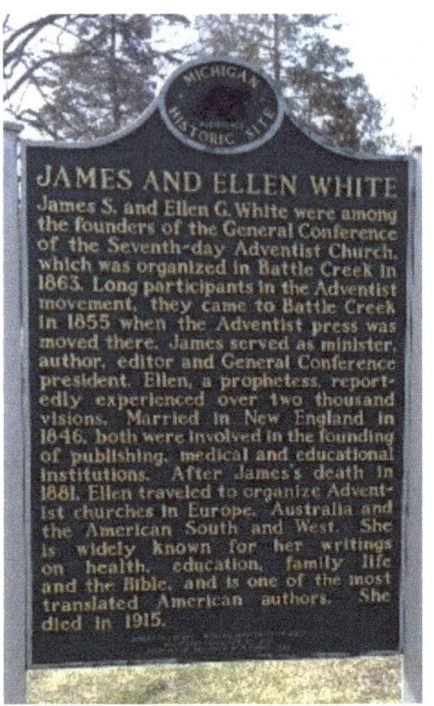

The buildings pictured below were a part of the original plantation property that was purchased during Ellen White's instruction to have a training school for colored students. The Old Mansion was a historic plantation home of the owner, Peter Blow, who was friends with former American President Andrew Jackson. It has been recorded that President Jackson visited Mr. Blow at the Old Mansion home. https://encyclopedia.adventist.org/article?id=AFWD During Mary Lou's matriculation at Oakwood, Mother Eugenia Cunningham lived at "Old Mansion". Mary Lou had many wonderful memories of visiting Mother Cunningham there.

"Old Mansion Residential Hall" (no longer in existence), 1896.

A slave cabin at Oakwood College, 1896.

Photo Credits: Mrs. Minneola Dixon, Loma Linda Article 1996

The Original Entrance of the Oakwood School founded in 1896.

Edson White was the Visionary Director of the Morning Star Mississippi Missionary Steamship. Edson was also the son of Ellen and James White.

Pictures of The Morning Star Missionary Steamship. All photos above are from the video, "Our Vision" https://maunaloaschool.org/vision

Great Grandmother Catherine (Evans) Battle became an Adventist because of Edson White's Mississippi Ministry. Her daughter Olivia (firstborn of 18) attended Oakwood. Olivia was Pearl's oldest sibling and Mary Lou's Aunt. Catherine was Pearl's Mother and Mary Lou's Grandmother.

As "6 generations" of Grandmother Catherine's children have been born to pass on her genetic torch to their children, it is now up to her remaining grandchildren, great grandchildren, her great, great grandchildren and now even great, great, great grandchildren, to pass on and take the truth that she found on The Morning Star Ship and shared with her 18 children. The Biblical Sabbath Truth that she found through yearning for more Bible Studies led her, by prayer, personal choice and the Holy Spirit to the acceptance of Seventh-day Adventism.

We can only imagine what her message would be to all her descendants today as we daily see the evidence of Matthew 24 happening right before our eyes. As Mary Lou received the Biblical Truths and passed on the torch to her children and students, we must also follow Mary Lou's Mindset of Determination, Courage and Faith to bless others.

In the following link, let us listen to This Old Spiritual, led under the direction of Dr. Eurydice Osterman and sung by the Oakwood College Choir. As it admonishes us to, "Walk Together Children", let us understand that we must realize that Grandma Catherine wouldn't want us to get weary because time is running out and she would want all of us to be part of that "Great Camp Meeting in the Promised Land." May this be the daily and Heavenward Goal not only for the Battle Family but also for everyone.

https://youtu.be/JQwBuwV8TE8?si=TCbJUTyb4X59-zPF

https://youtu.be/JQwBuwV8TE8?si=TqgApTi8ilm6ufRK

Felix and Catherine Battle's Four Generation of Descendants. Top Row, left to right: Felix Battle, Catherine (Evans) Battle, Pearl Battle, Mary Louise Battle Middle Row, left to right: Hubert Dale Washington, Marla Lynne (2nd & 3rd photos), Michelle Linda Washington (4th. picture) Third Row, Danielle Washington, Jonathan Washington, Miya Thomas (3rd. & 4th. photos)

Special Thanks

Tracey Betts Williams   **Mary Lou & Hubert D. Washington**

Thank you Tracey and Hubert for your editing and suggestions along the seven-year process of this project. I want to especially thank Tracey for sharing her expertise, time and talents with guiding me over the phone to my journey with Google Docs. Thank you both also for your personal donations.

Additionally, I thank you Tracey for sending me a brand new Chrome Book to make this process easier, while trying to get me away from typing this manuscript on my phone. Continued blessings to you, my teacher friend and my brother, Hubert.

Last, but certainly not least, I thank Edward Green who encouraged me to persevere until I fully completed this project and had all aspects of the manuscript finished. His prayerful, financial and spiritual support were extremely crucial during the last leg of this literary journey. May God's blessings continue to keep you also, Eddie.

Edward Green, Sr.

Blessed is the one who perseveres under trial because, having stood the test, that person will receive the crown of life that the Lord has promised to those who love him. James 1: 12

REMEMBERING YOU

I remember the days of long ago and the brilliance of your smile.
The joy in your laugh, the peace in your voice has carried me from mile to mile.
You gave your last on so many days to make sure that I'd be okay.
No matter what the sacrifice was, you always found a way.

I remember the way you carried your pain on the darkest days of your life.
You were strong like a flint upholding your vows each time that you were a wife.
Through sickness, death, through better and worse, you were a faithful lady.
Though many a tongue wagged all about you, you never chose to be shady.

I remember your heart as it beat through cancer. I remember how you always prayed.
There was never a fear as you trusted the Master. Your faith in God was laid.
You never let go of your favorite hymns.
Your faith in your Lord was never dim.
I remember how you walked this earthly sod.
Your hope was truly in God.

I remember the way that you stood your ground to help anyone that you could.
You stood up with courage and never backed down because you felt that you should.
The work that you did was honest and true.
The virtue you shared had its own special hue.
I remember the way you loved shades of blue.
I can not stop remembering you.

I remember the dignity of your grace and how you uplifted others.
Though you were not perfect, you were perfectly happy to be our lovely Mother.
The depth of your heart was truly deep.
Your kindness never went to sleep.
All the love that you gave, you soon will reap, when Jesus comes one day.
Safe in Heaven you will stay.

I remember you my faithful Mother regardless of your death.
You were the one who gave me life and felt my very first breath.
Though many years have come and gone, the love that you shared still lingers on.
I can never stop remembering you,
"A True Matriarch, Mary Lou".

In Memory of Mary Lou Hemingway
May 10, 2020

Only God Can

Michelle Washington

Mary Lou's Mindset was a result of her faithful trust in God. May all of us realize and claim that **"Only God Can"** do what is needed at any time within our lives.

God is able. He is a miracle working God. We all can choose to trust God now.

Mary Lou's 1947 Official Oakwood Graduation Photo

"Remember that you will never reach a higher standard than you yourself set. Then set your mark high, and step by step, even though it be by painful effort, by self-denial and sacrifice, ascend the whole length of the ladder of progress. Let nothing hinder you."

Messages to Young People, page 99, by Ellen G. White

If you or your organization is desirous of more information regarding book signings, book readings, group presentations or any other information related to Mary Lou's Mindset, you may share your communication at the following email.

marylousmindset@gmail.com

In addition, the family of Dr. Mary Lou (Battle - Washington) Hemingway will be announcing and launching a scholarship in her name for Oakwood University Students majoring in Business.

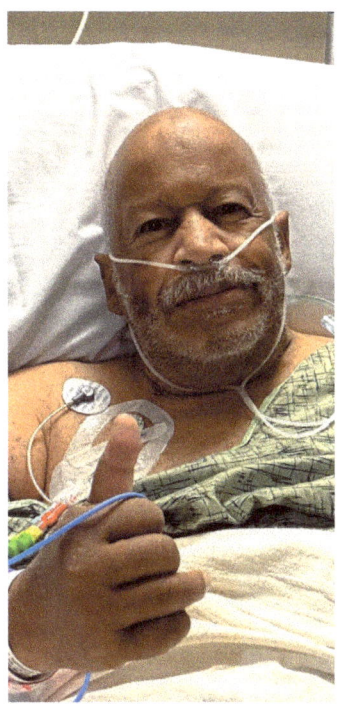

On November 18, 2024, my one and only brother, who also was my "big brother" passed away. Hubert Dale Washington "HUE", was a huge part of making sure that our Mother's Book was published. He prayerfully encouraged me every step of the way. Even all the way up to the last week of his ability to speak.

It is with these thoughts that I place this memorial dedication page in his memory.

I am thankful for everything that he shared to encourage me with, **Mary Lou's Mindset.**

Until Jesus comes,

   Rest in Peace, Big Brother...

GOOD BYE FOR NOW, MY BIG BROTHER

Good bye for now, my Big Brother.
You have really been a true friend.
Though you will now be resting,
Thoughts of you will never end.

You fought a fearless fight.
You were tired of so many things.
For all that you bravely endured,
God will give you your heavenly wings.

So many people loved you, because you had a huge heart.
You never met a stranger.
Loving kindness was where you would start.

What an honor and a blessing to have walked with you, my Big Brother.
Like a guardian angel from Heaven,
you loved Marla and I like no other.

Everywhere that you ever went, you always gave your best.
Though "some" took your love for granted,
God counted your motives as blessed.

My "Hubie", I'll ever cherish the deep depths of our sibling bond.
No one can ever diminsh all that we've shared from Toledo and beyond.

Rest well, my beloved brother.

You have been one of the great men.

"Who can deny the love you have shown?"

There is not one tounge, nor one pen.

I'm so glad that our parents are resting.

They could not have carried your death.

When God lifts you from the grave,

He will give you your "second breath".

You will be well missed "Hubert Dale", from one coast to another.

When Jesus soon returns, we'll never part again my "Big Brother".

Written for: My one & only brother, Hubert Dale Washington

Written on:December 16, 2024

By: *Michelle Washington*

www.ingramcontent.com/pod-product-compliance
Lightning Source LLC
Chambersburg PA
CBHW051135120626
46547CB00012B/813